37 THEATRE SONGS FOR SOPRANO

ISBN-13: 978-1-4234-2398-0
ISBN-10: 1-4234-2398-4

Visit Hal Leonard Online at
www.halleonard.com

FOREWORD

An ingénue is broadly defined as a fairly innocent, pretty young woman. It is as common in theatre as any character type, with roots that go back to the Greeks. Such characters abound in Shakespeare. And the tradition is by no means over. Ingénue characters can be constantly spotted in movies and on television as well as in plays and musicals. On the musical stage such characters have roots in the soubrettes and romantic leads of opera, or in the leading female roles in French operettas by Offenbach, English operettas by Gilbert and Sullivan, in zarzuelas, or in Viennese operettas.

Some ingénue characters are static throughout a story, with no fundamental transformation. Others go through some struggle or crisis and evolve to more worldliness. Ingénues can be single or married young women. Some are quite serious by temperament; some are mischievous; others show a more comic or flirtatious side. Ingénues can be light characters who simply grace the story with their presence and charm, or they can be more complex young women who show deeper emotions. But they always retain an essentially lyrical, feminine quality.

In musical theatre traditions the ingénue is typically a soprano (although it does happen that ingénues are occasionally belters). This collection is a sampling of soprano songs from many ingénue roles. Among the most famous are Kim MacAfee in *Bye Bye Birdie*, Guenevere in *Camelot*, Julie Jordan in *Carousel*, the title character in *Cinderella*, Luisa in *The Fantasticks*, Sarah Brown in *Guys and Dolls*, Cosette in *Les Misérables*, Marion Paroo in *The Music Man*, Eliza Doolittle in *My Fair Lady*, Laurey in *Oklahoma!*, Christine Daaé in *The Phantom of the Opera*, Magnolia Ravenal in *Show Boat*, and Maria (and Liesel too) in *The Sound of Music*.

There have been many well-known ingénue sopranos on Broadway and in movie musicals. To name a few: Julie Andrews, Barbara Cook, Shirley Jones, Jane Powell, Kathryn Grayson, Deanna Durbin, Rebecca Luker, Sarah Brightman, and Kristin Chenoweth.

Contrary to popular belief, portraying an ingénue is not necessarily easy on stage. It can be much easier as an actress to play a character with more edge, or more idiosyncrasies to hide behind. The eternal challenge is how to find an interesting way to play an ingénue, or sing such a character's song, so that the result is not standard-issue bland, but has some spark of life and individuality.

In other words, portraying an ingénue in song requires all the same creative imagination and investigation as any other acting assignment. Using her song as a guide, you must find her spirit and the details that make her unique.

Do you have an ingénue inside you, to breathe new life into these wonderful songs? You don't have to wonder "Wouldn't It Be Loverly." Just choose a song and begin to "Make Believe."

Richard Walters
editor

CONTENTS

PAGE	TITLE	SHOW	CD ONE ACCOMPANIMENT TRACK NO.
4	And This Is My Beloved[3]	KISMET	1
7	Another Suitcase in Another Hall[6]	EVITA	2
12	The Girl in 14 G*[5]		3
28	Goodnight, My Someone[6]	THE MUSIC MAN	4
32	How Lovely to Be a Woman[4]	BYE BYE BIRDIE	5
23	I Could Be Happy with You[6]	THE BOY FRIEND	6
40	I Could Have Danced All Night[3]	MY FAIR LADY	7
50	I Have Dreamed[5]	THE KING AND I	8
54	I Loved You Once in Silence[5]	CAMELOT	9
47	I'll Know[1]	GUYS AND DOLLS	10
58	If I Loved You[1]	CAROUSEL	11
62	In My Life[6]	LES MISÉRABLES	12
64	In My Own Little Corner[5]	CINDERELLA	13
71	Is It Really Me?[1]	110 IN THE SHADE	14
74	It Wonders Me[5]	PLAIN AND FANCY	15
79	Lovely[5]	A FUNNY THING HAPPENED ON THE WAY TO THE FORUM	16
84	Make Believe[6]	SHOW BOAT	17
89	Many a New Day[3]	OKLAHOMA!	18
			CD TWO
94	Much More[3]	THE FANTASTICKS	1
100	My Favorite Things[2]	THE SOUND OF MUSIC	2
104	My White Knight[5]	THE MUSIC MAN	3
108	No Other Love[1]	ME AND JULIET	4
111	Once You Lose Your Heart[5]	ME AND MY GIRL	5
116	Out of My Dreams[3]	OKLAHOMA!	6
122	The Simple Joys of Maidenhood[5]	CAMELOT	7
129	Simple Little Things[4]	110 IN THE SHADE	8
134	Sixteen Going on Seventeen[2]	THE SOUND OF MUSIC	9
137	So Many People[5]	SATURDAY NIGHT	10
142	The Sound of Music[5]	THE SOUND OF MUSIC	11
147	There's a Small Hotel[4]	ON YOUR TOES	12
154	Think of Me[4]	THE PHANTOM OF THE OPERA	13
166	Till There Was You[3]	THE MUSIC MAN	14
170	We Kiss in a Shadow[1]	THE KING AND I	15
174	What's the Use of Wond'rin'[6]	CAROUSEL	16
178	Wishing You Were Somehow Here Again[6]	THE PHANTOM OF THE OPERA	17
161	Without You[4]	MY FAIR LADY	18
182	Wouldn't It Be Loverly[1]	MY FAIR LADY	19

* This song, recorded by Kristin Chenoweth on ***Let Yourself Go***, is not from a show.

Pianists on the CDs: [1] Brian Dean [2] Louise Lerch [3] Sue Malmberg [4] Ruben Piirainen [5] Christopher Ruck [6] Richard Walters

AND THIS IS MY BELOVED

from *Kismet*

Music and Lyrics by
Robert Wright and George Forrest
(based on themes of Alexander Borodin)

Andantino

p

MARSINAH:

Dawn's prom-is-ing skies, Pet-als on a pool drift - ing; I - mag-ine these ____ in one pair of eyes, And this is my be - lov - ed.

Strange spice from the south, Hon-ey through the comb

sift - ing; I - mag-ine these on one ea-ger mouth,
And this is my be - lov - ed.
Poco più mosso
And when he speaks,
And when he talks to me, Mu - sic! Mys - ter-y!
mf
And when he moves And when he walks with me, Par - a-dise comes sud-den-ly

Poco stentato
ten.
near!
All that can stir,
All that can stun,
ten.
f
ten.
All that's for the heart's
lift - ing;
I - mag-ine these in
mp
mf
one per-fect one,
And this is my be - lov - ed!
And this is my be - lov - ed!
f
8va
loco
L.H.
cresc.

ANOTHER SUITCASE IN ANOTHER HALL

from *Evita*

Lyrics by Tim Rice
Music by Andrew Lloyd Webber

It would be stylistically appropriate for the pianist to improvise an accompaniment.

C/G F C F/G C
all the same I hate it, would - n't you? So what hap-pens now? So what hap-pens

F/G C F Am
now? Where am I go-ing to? Where am I

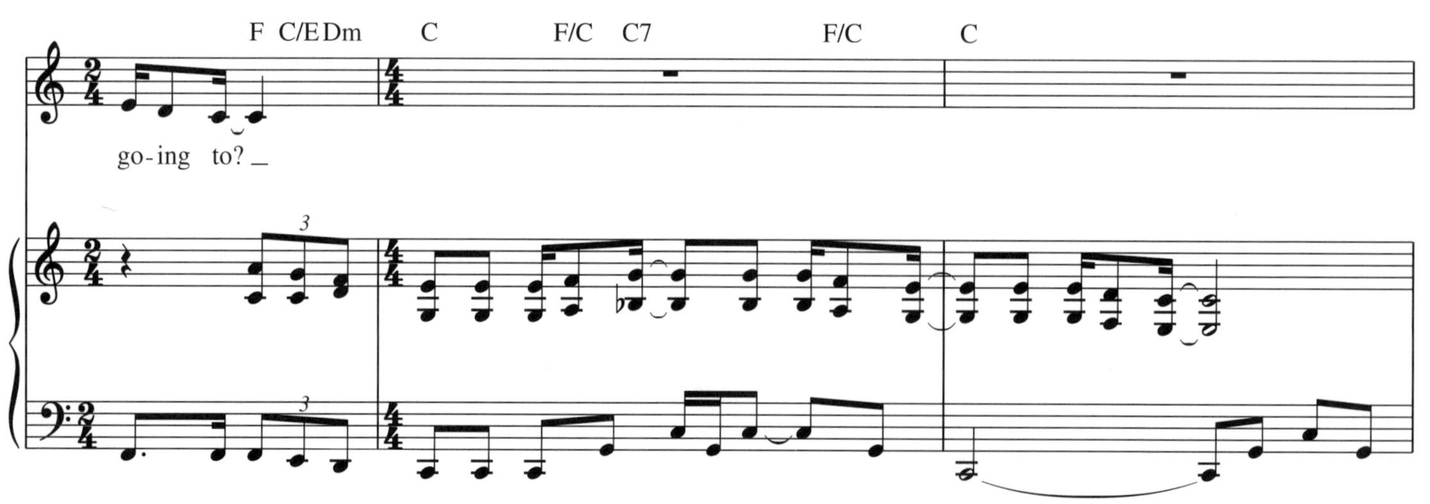
F C/E Dm C F/C C7 F/C C
go-ing to?

C F G7 C F C/E Dm G
Time and time a - gain I've said that I don't care; That I'm im- mune to gloom, that I'm

C G7 C F G Am
hard __ through and through: But ev - 'ry time it mat- ters all my words de - sert me; So

C/G F C F/G F C
an - y - one can hurt me and they do. So what hap-pens now? So what hap-pens

F/G
C
F
Am
now? Where am I go-ing to? Where am I
F
C/E Dm
C
go-ing to?
F
G7
C
Call in three months' time and I'll be fine I know; Well
F
C/E
Dm
G
C
G7
C
F
may-be not that fine, but I'll sur-vive an-y-how: I won't re-call the names and plac-es

G
Am
C/G
F
C
of this sad oc - ca - sion; But that's no con - so - la - tion, here and now. So what hap - pens

F/G
C7
F/G
F
C7
now? So what hap - pens now? Where am I

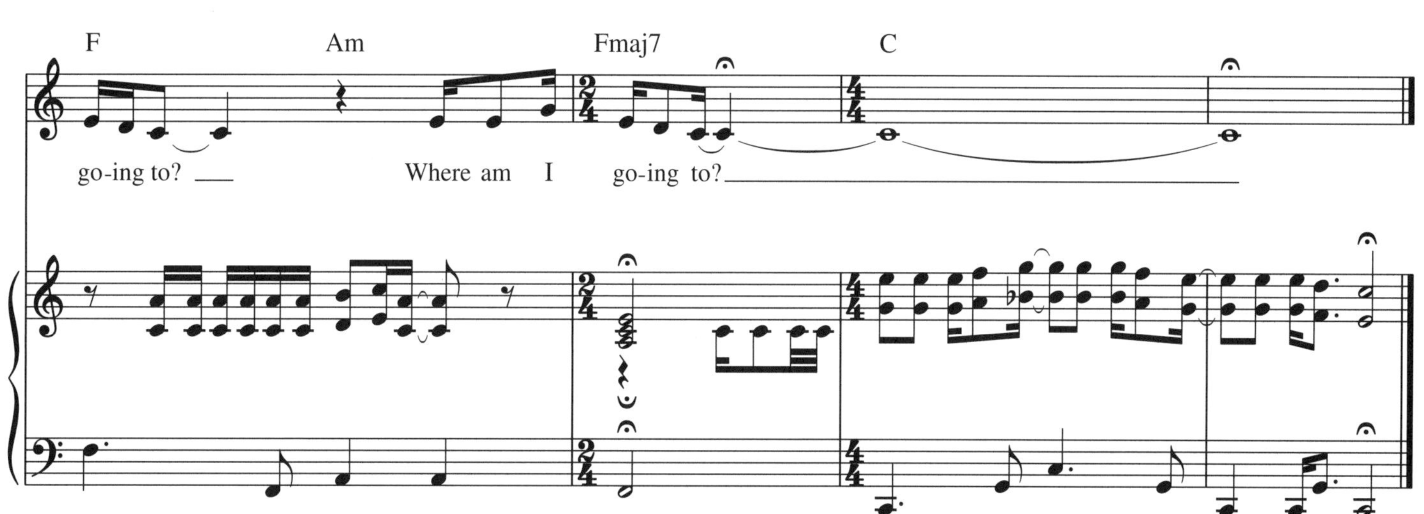
F
Am
Fmaj7
C
go - ing to? Where am I go - ing to?

THE GIRL IN 14G

Music by Jeanine Tesori
Lyrics by Dick Scanlan

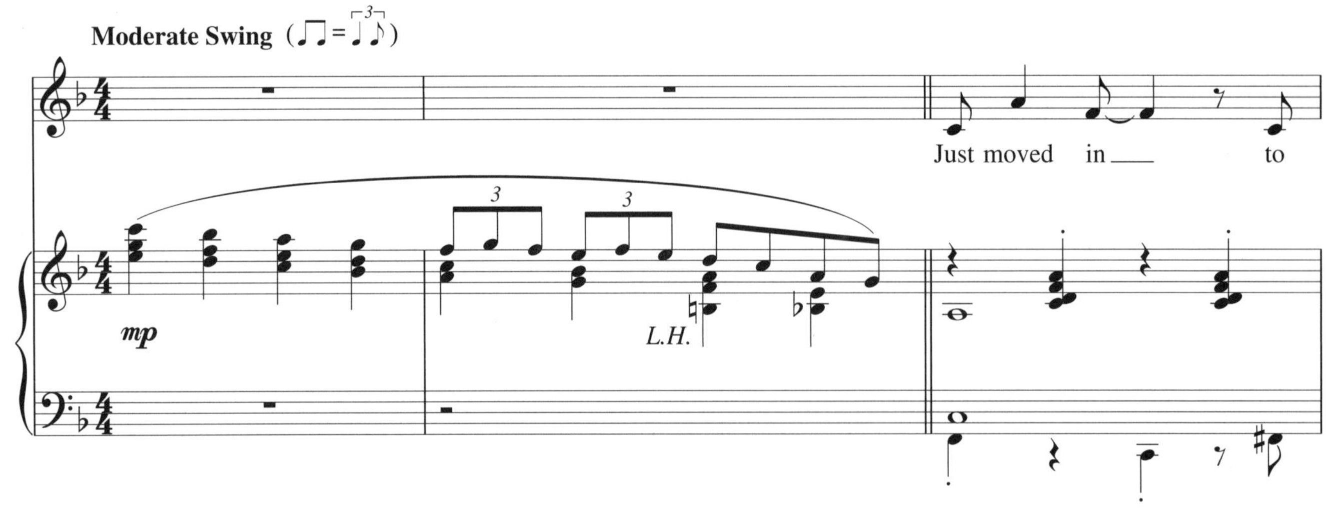

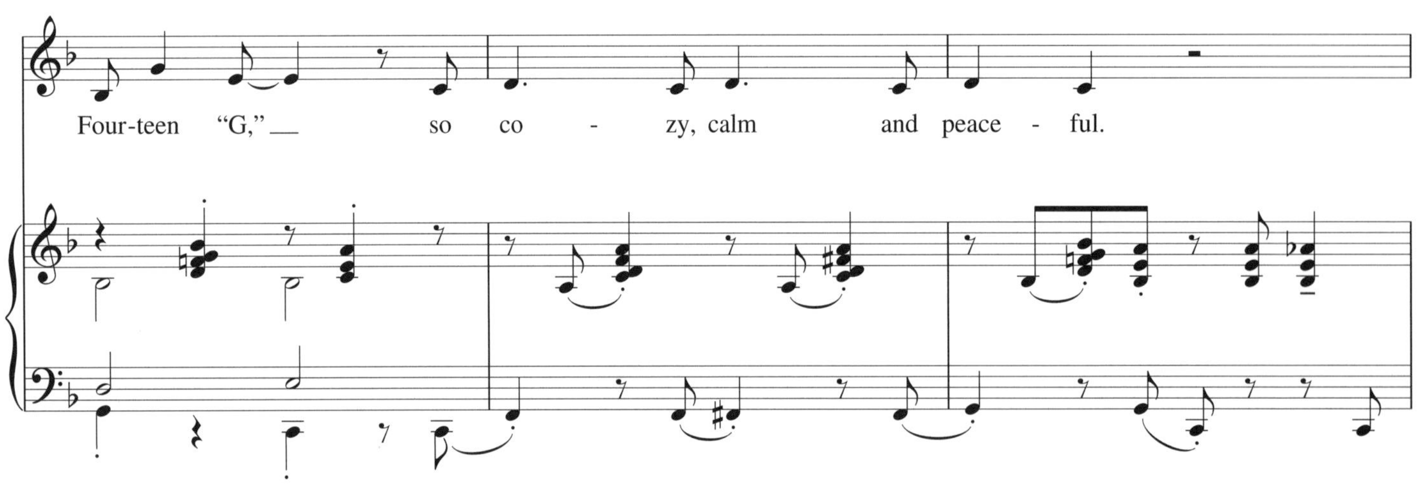

Pets are banned, parties too, and no so-li-ci-ta-tions.
mf
Win-dow seat with gar-den view.
No swing
A per-fect nook to read a book. I'm lost in my Jane Aus-ten when I
L.H.
mp
decresc. poco a poco
hear:
À la "Tristan" (no swing)
"Ah, ah."
ff
faster

Tempo I (Swing)
Say it is - n't so. Not the flat be -
sub. p
low. From an op - 'ra wan - na be___ in
Thir - teen "G,"___ a mat - i - nee of some can - ta - ta, Wag-ner's Ring and Tra - vi - a - ta.
mp
Faster, à la "Magic Flute" (no swing)
"Ah, ah, ah, ah, ah, ah, ah, ah, ah, ah, ah, ah, ah, ah, ah, ah, ah, ah, ah, ah, ah, ah, ah,
ff mf

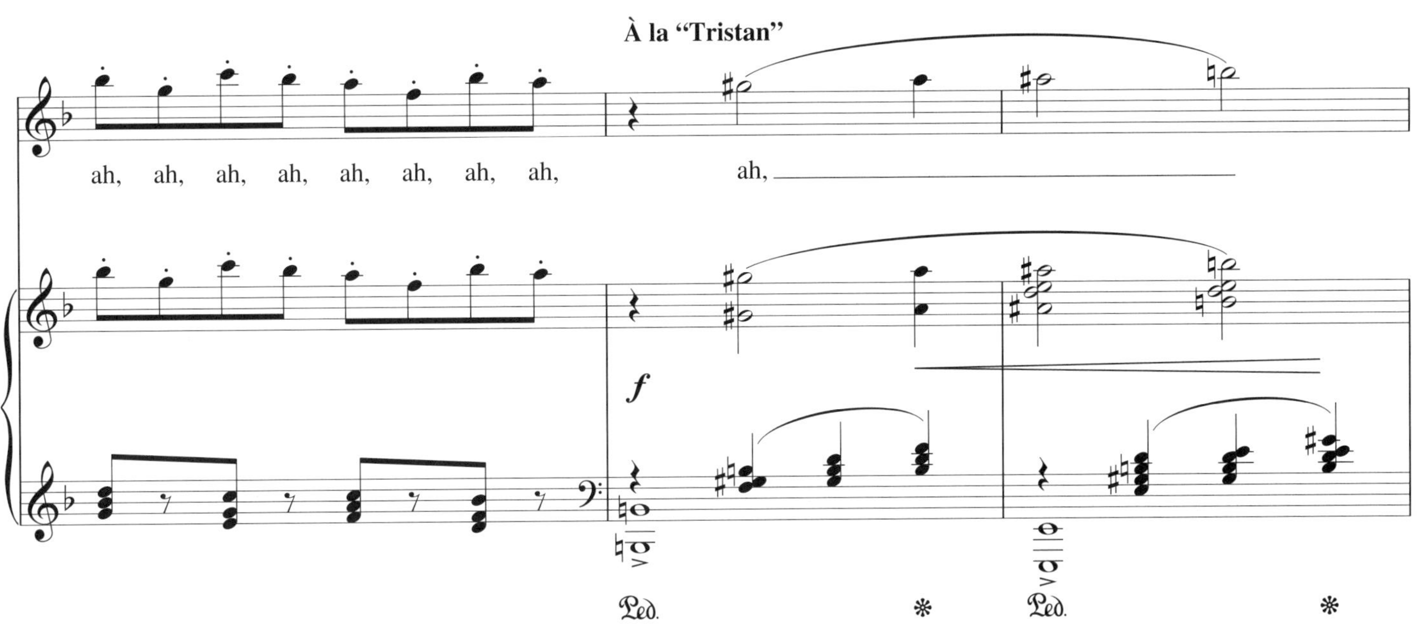
À la "Tristan"
ah, ah, ah, ah, ah, ah, ah, ah,
ah,
f
Ped.
Ped.

À la "Magic Flute"
tr
tr
ah, ah, ah, ah, ah,
ah, ah, ah, ah, ah,
ah, ah, ah, ah, ah, ah, ah, ah,
mf

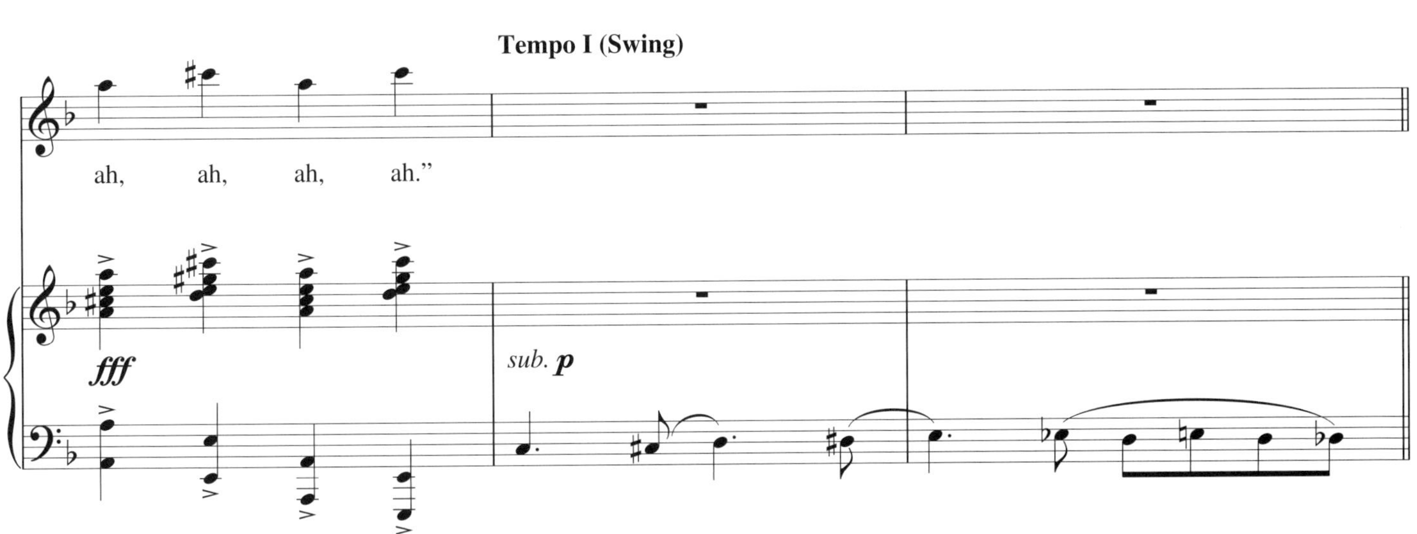
Tempo I (Swing)
ah, ah, ah, ah."
fff
sub. p

My first night in Four-teen "G." I'll put up with Puc - ci - ni. Brew my - self a cup of tea.
sim.
Cro - chet un - til she's *fi* - *ni.* Half past eight,
mf
not a peep ex - cept the clock tick tock - in'.

No swing
Now I lay me down to sleep. A com - fy bed
L.H.
mp
to rest my head. A stretch, a yawn; I'm al - most gone, then
rit. e dim.
R.H.
Fast Jazz, à la Ella Fitzgerald (Swing)
"Doo - wee - zwah doo -
f
tah - dup - doo spee-di-lee dee - floy - doy bee - blip,

opt.
naa - naa - naa - naa - naa - naa - naa - naa - naa - naa - naa - naa,
woo - weeee.
Tempo I
Now the girl up - stairs
wakes me un - a -
sub. p
wares.
Blow - in' down from
Fif - teen "G" her
rev - eil - le.
She's scat - tin' like her name is El - la. Guess who an - swers a cap - pel - la.
mp
lightly

Fast Jazz ("Ella")
Operatic
"Zoot doo doot floy doy." "Ah."
f
mf molto legato
Fast Jazz ("Ella")
Operatic
"Zoot doo doot floy dee doy." "Ah."
f
mf molto legato
Somewhat freely
I'm not one to raise my voice, make a fuss or speak my mind, but
sub. mp
Rubato
Slower
might I quer - y... Would you mind if... Could you kind - ly... stop!
poco accel.
pp
ppp
colla voce

Fast March
staccato
cresc. poco a poco
"That felt good" Stop!
f
Broad Swing
Thir - teen, Fif - teen,
ff
molto rit.
Four-teen "G." A most un - like - ly tri - o.

Operatic
Not quite three - part har - mo - ny.
3
All day, all night we're sing - in':
Fast Jazz
"Zoot doo doot floy doy a zee bop boo doo
boy ta boy."
"Stop!"
"Ah.

Broad swing
Ah."
Had my fill
of peace and qui - et. Shout out loud. I've
changed my di - et, all be - cause of Four - teen "G!"
rit.

I COULD BE HAPPY WITH YOU

from *The Boy Friend*

Words and Music by
Sandy Wilson

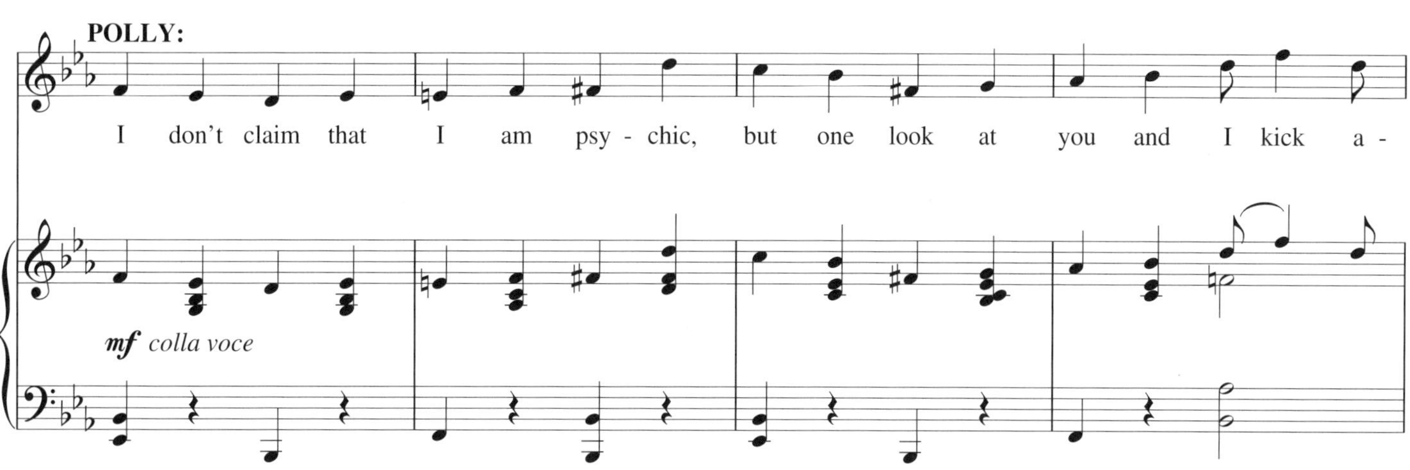

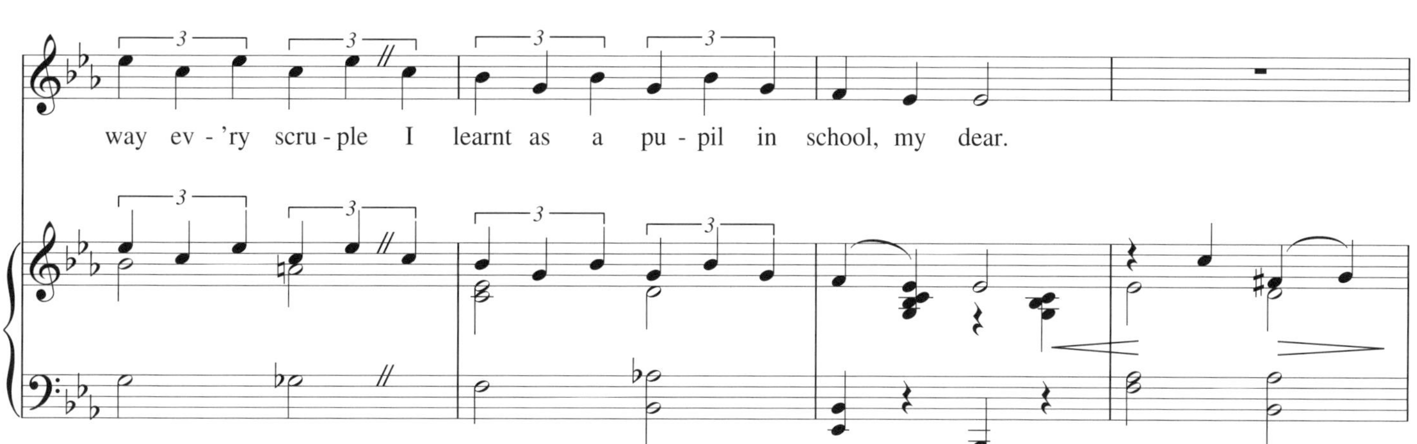

I'm not one to make pre - dic - tions, but I've thrown off all re - stric-tions And
don't mind con - fess - ing I think it's a bless - ing That you are here.
Though I'm pre - pared to find I'm wrong, I've
legato
got a fun - ny feel - ing we be - long To - geth - er.
rall.
rall.

(Not too fast)
I could be hap - py with you If
mf a tempo
you could be hap - py with me.
I'd be con - tent - ed to live an - y - where,
What would I care,
rall.
As long as you were there?
rall.

a tempo
Skies may not al - ways be blue,
But
mf a tempo
one thing is clear as can be,
I know that
I could be hap - py with you, My dar - ling.
If
you could be hap - py with me.

Skies may not al - ways be blue,
But
one thing is clear as can be.
I know that
I could be hap - py with you,
My dar - ling,
If
you could be hap - py with me.
pp

GOODNIGHT, MY SOMEONE

from Meredith Willson's *The Music Man*

By Meredith Willson

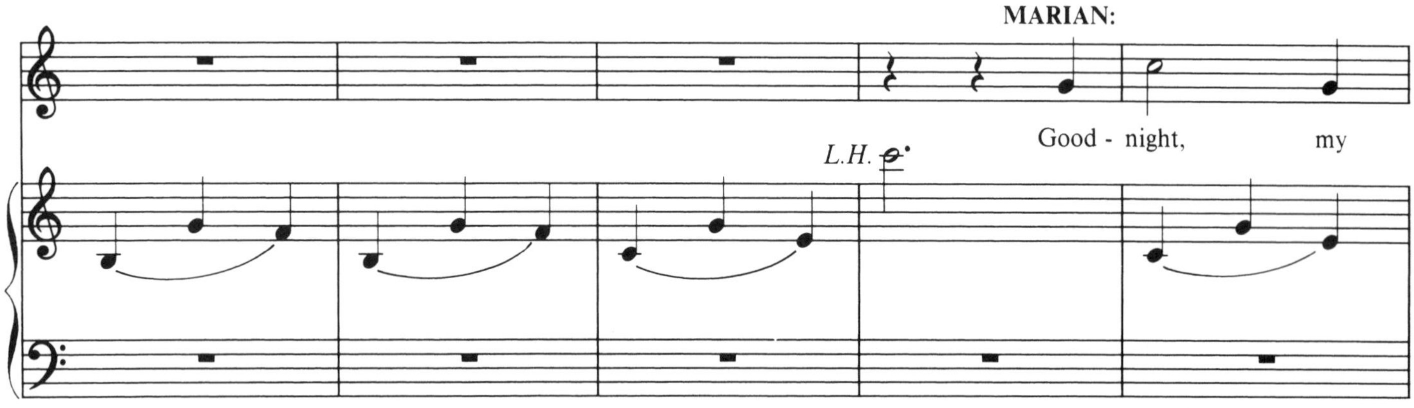

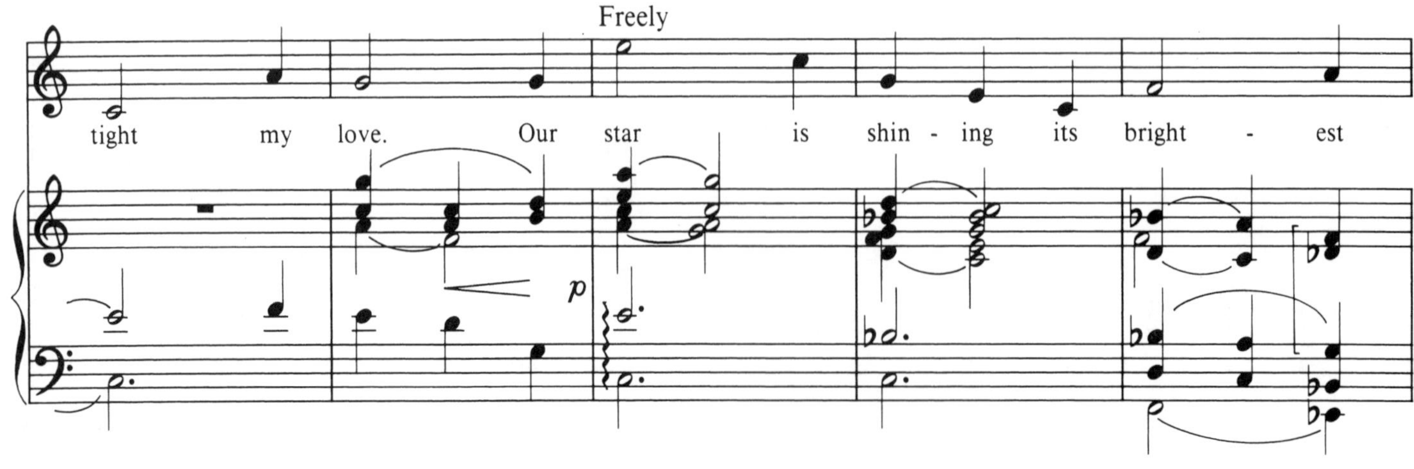

light for good - night, my love, for good - night. Sweet
dreams be yours, dear, if dreams there be; Sweet dreams to
L.H.
car - ry you close to me. I wish they may, and I
wish they might. Now good-night, my some - one, good - night.
L.H.

Poco mosso
8va
True love can be whis - pered from heart to heart, when
lov - ers are part - ed they say.
8va
L.H.
But I must de -
poco rit.
pend on a wish and a star, as long as my heart does - n't
poco rit.
Tempo I
know who you are. Sweet dreams be yours, dear, if dreams there
pp

be. Sweet dreams to car - ry you close to
me. I wish they may, and I wish they
ten.
poco meno
might. Now good-night, my some - one, good - night Good -
ten.
ten.
ten.
colla parte
night. Good - night.
L.H.
pp

HOW LOVELY TO BE A WOMAN

from *Bye Bye Birdie*

Lyric by Lee Adams
Music by Charles Strouse

have that hap - py, grown up, fe - male feel - ing!
8va
loco
p a tempo
How love - ly to be a wom - an! The
wait was well worth - while, how love - ly to

8va
wear mas - ca - ra, and smile a wom - an's
smile. How love - ly to have a fig - ure
That's round in - stead of flat, When -
ev - er you hear boys whis - tle You're what they're

whis - tling at! It's won - der - ful to feel
The way a wom - an feels, It
gives you such a glow Just to know You're
wear - ing lip - stick and heels. How love - ly to
3
3

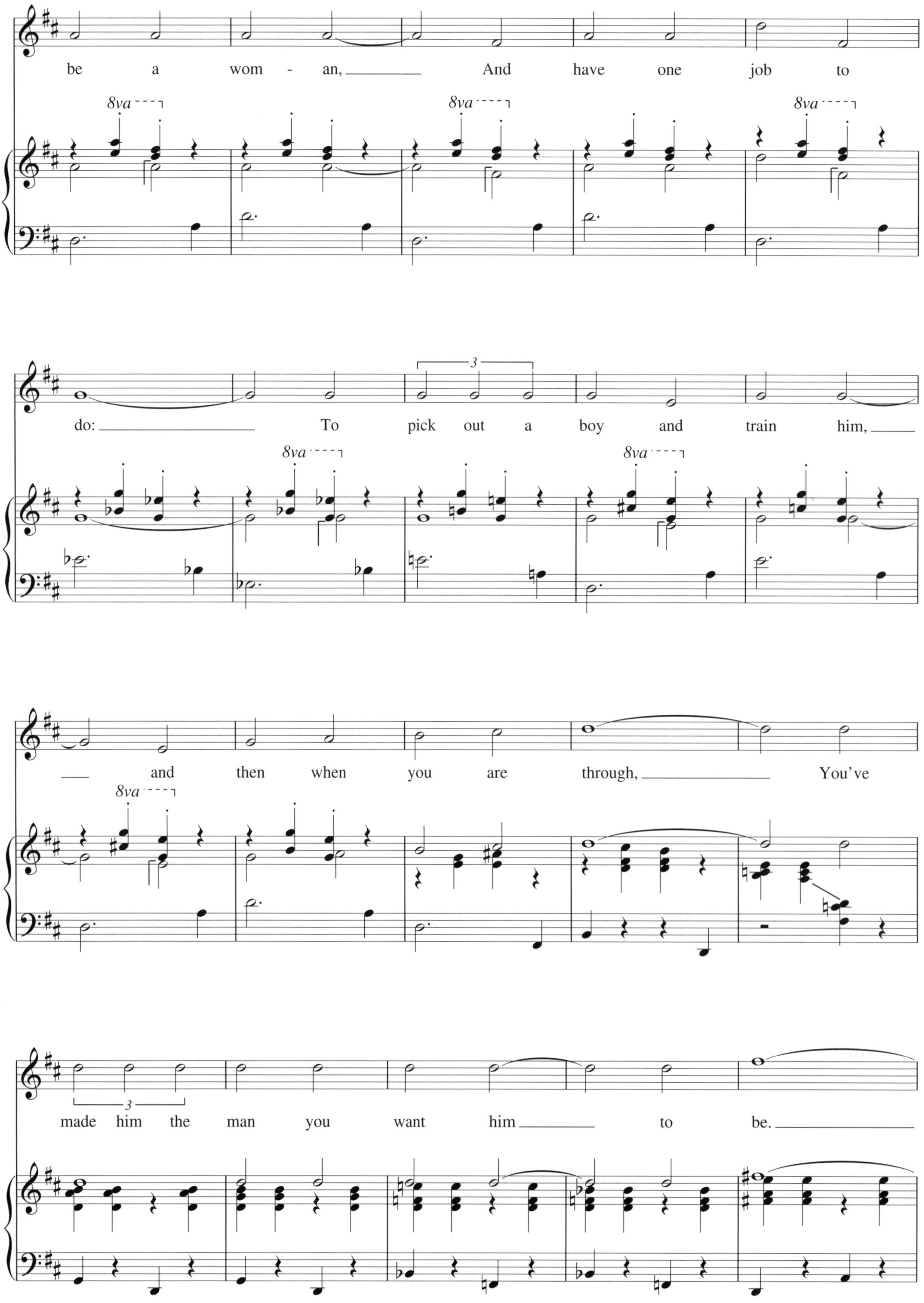

be a wom - an, And have one job to

8va

do: To pick out a boy and train him,

3

8va

— and then when you are through, You've

8va

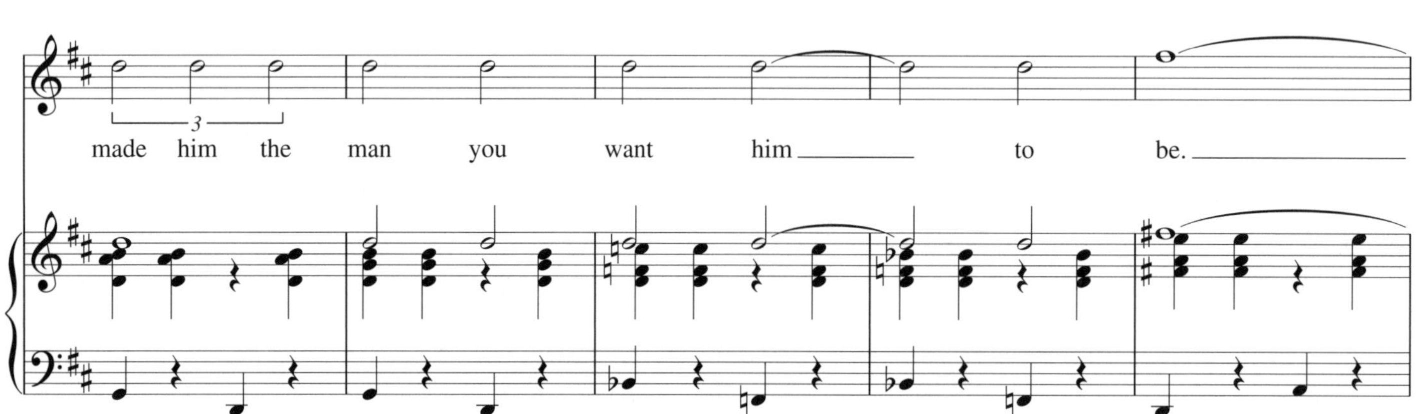

Life's love - ly when you're a
wom - an like me!
How
won - der - ful to know
The things a wom - an
knows!
How mar - ve - lous to wait

For a date In sim - ply beau - ti - ful
clothes! How love - ly to be a wom - an
And change from boys to men! To
go to a fan - cy night club, And stay out
3
8va

af - ter ten! How love - ly to be so
grown - up and free!
con rubato
Life's love - ly when you're a wom - an
a tempo
like me!
a tempo
8va

I COULD HAVE DANCED ALL NIGHT

from *My Fair Lady*

Words by Alan Jay Lerner
Music by Frederick Loewe

could - n't sleep to - night!
Not for all the
jew - els in the crown!
I could have
p
danced all night!
I could have danced all
night! And still have begged for

more.
I could have spread my
wings
And done a thou - sand things I've
nev - er done be - fore.
I'll nev - er know what made it so ex -

cit - ing; Why all at once my

heart took flight. I on - ly

ten. ten. ten.

f

know when he be-gan to dance with

me, I could have danced, danced, danced, All

mp

L'istesso tempo
pp
night!
I could have
mf
dim.
pp
danced
all
night!
I could have danced
all
night!
And
still
have
begged
for
more.
I could have spread
my

wings
And done a thou - sand things
I've
nev - er done
be - fore.
I'll nev - er know
what made it so
ex -
cit - ing;
Why all at once
my

heart
took
flight.
I
on - ly
mf
(non rit.)
know
when
he
be - gan to dance
with
cresc.
me,
I could have danced,
danced,
danced
f
8vb
all
night!
f
ff

I'LL KNOW

from *Guys and Dolls*

By Frank Loesser

Adapted as a solo here, the song is a duet scene for Sarah and Sky in the show.

(with mounting determination)
run to his arms that at last I've come home safe and sound and till then I shall
rit.
wait and till then I'll be strong for I'll know when my
ten.
love comes a - long.
I won't take a chance, my

love will be just what I need not some fly - by - night Broad - way ro -
mance, and till then I shall wait and till
then I'll be strong for I'll know when my
love comes a - long.
accel.
f

I HAVE DREAMED

from *The King and I*

Lyrics by Oscar Hammerstein II
Music by Richard Rodgers

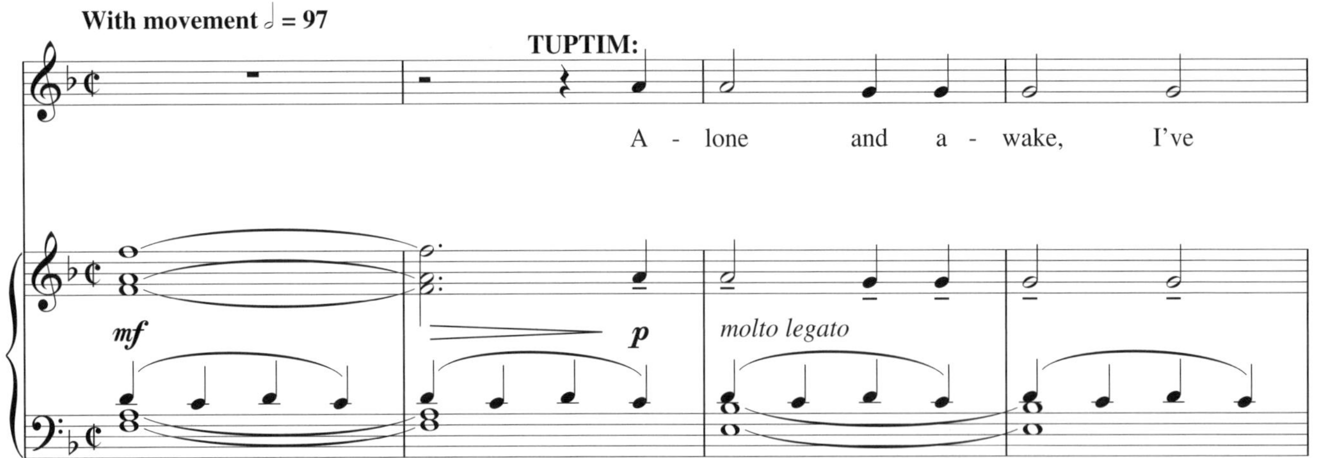

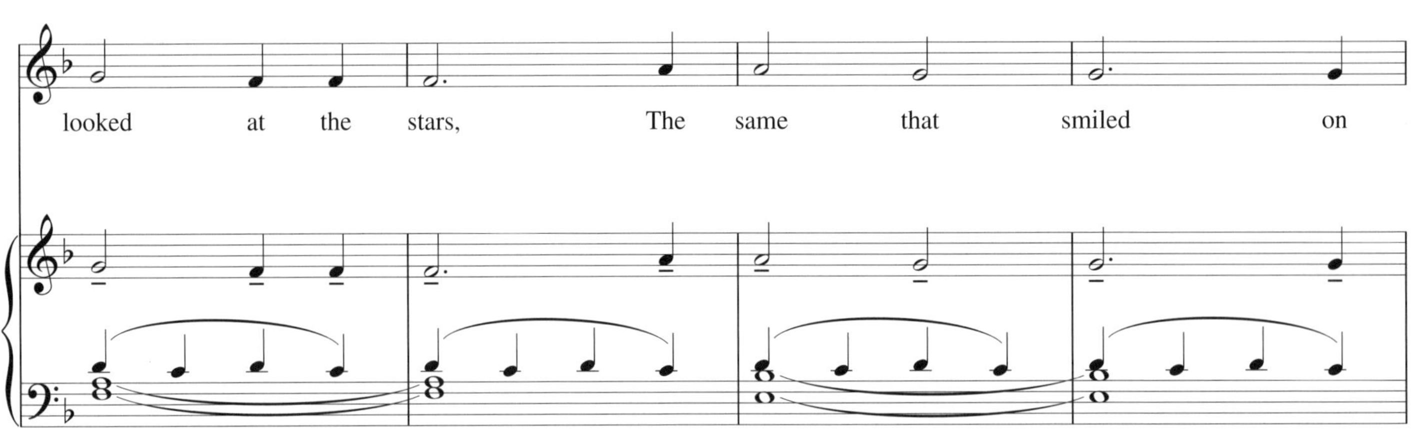

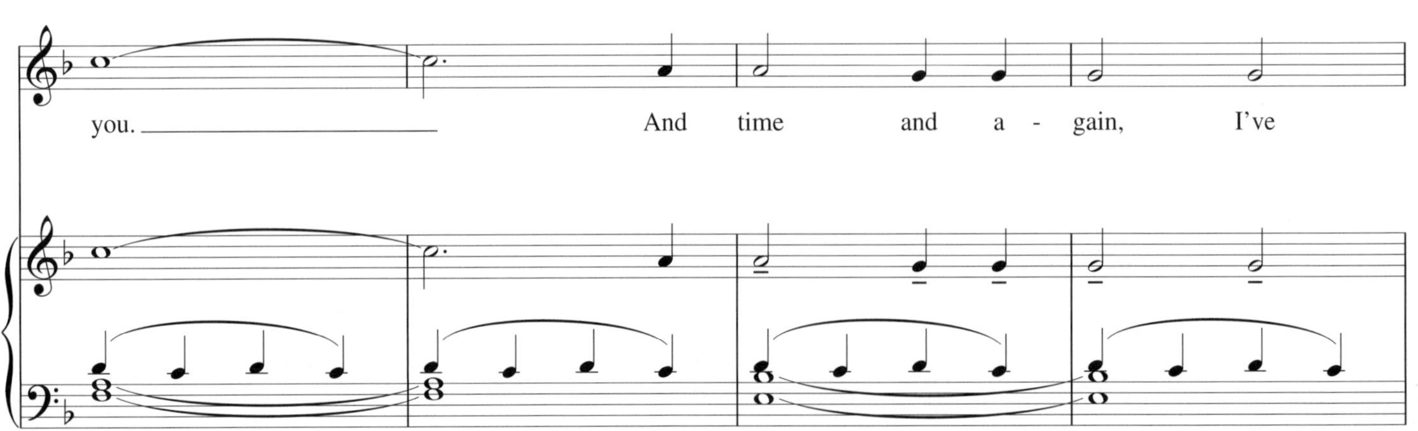

thought all the things that you were think - ing
too.
Slowly 𝅗𝅥 = 60
rit.
a tempo
I have dreamed
p
rit.
p a tempo
that your arms are love - ly,
I have dreamed what a joy you'll be.

I have dreamed ev - 'ry word you'll
whis - per, When you're close,
close to me.
How you look
in the glow of eve - ning,

I have dreamed and en - joyed the view.
In these dreams I've loved you so That by now I think I
mf passionately
know What it's like to be loved by you,
cresc.
f allargando
High Shelf
molto rit.
I will love be - ing loved by you.
molto rit.
ff

I LOVED YOU ONCE IN SILENCE

from *Camelot*

Words by Alan Jay Lerner
Music by Frederick Loewe

All the while not know - ing You loved me too.
Yes, loved me in lone - some si - lence;
Your heart filled with dark des- pair... Think-ing
love would flame in you for - ev - er, And I'd nev - er,

(Mosso)
nev - er know the flame was there. Then one
day we cast a - way our se - cret long - ing; The rag - ing
(Tempo I)
tide we held in - side would hold no more. The si - lence
dolce
at last was bro - ken! We flung wide our pris - on

door.
Ev - 'ry joy - ous word of love was spo - ken...
poco rit.
rall.
Andante
And now there's twice as much grief, Twice the strain for us, Twice the des -
rall.
colla voce
sfz
pair, Twice the pain for us As we had known
be - fore.
poco rubato
pp

IF I LOVED YOU

from *Carousel*

Lyrics by Oscar Hammerstein II
Music by Richard Rodgers

warp 'd get mixed with the woof If I
loved you. But
Broadly
some-how I ken see just ex - ack - ly how I'd be.
ppp
Moderato espressivo
If I loved you, Time and a - gain I would try to say
3
3
pp

All I'd want you to know.
3
3
3
3
If I loved you, Words would-n't come in an eas - y way.
3
3
Round in cir - cles I'd go!
3
3
3
Long - in' to tell you, but a - fraid and shy,
p

I let my gold - en chan - ces pass me by!
Soon you'd leave me, off you would go in the mist of day,
Nev - er, nev - er to know
How I loved you, If I loved you!

IN MY LIFE

from *Les Misérables*

Music by Claude-Michel Schönberg
Lyrics by Herbert Kretzmer
Original Text by Alain Boublil and Jean-Marc Natel

way, wait-ing for me.
Does he know I'm a-live? Do I know if he's

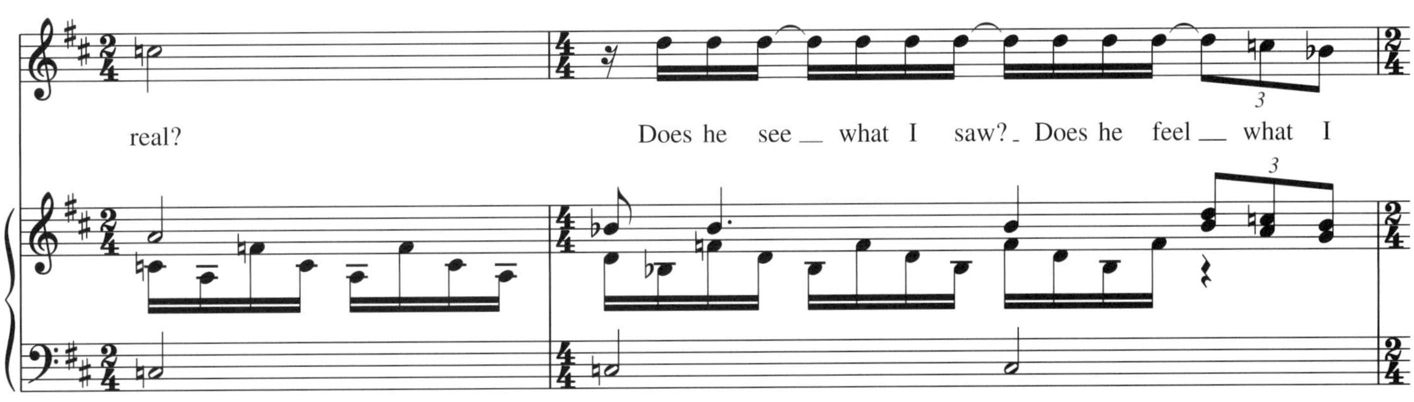
real?
Does he see what I saw? Does he feel what I

feel? In my life I'm no lon-ger a - lone. Now the love of my life is so

near. Find me now. Find me here.

IN MY OWN LITTLE CORNER

from *Cinderella*

Lyrics by Oscar Hammerstein II
Music by Richard Rodgers

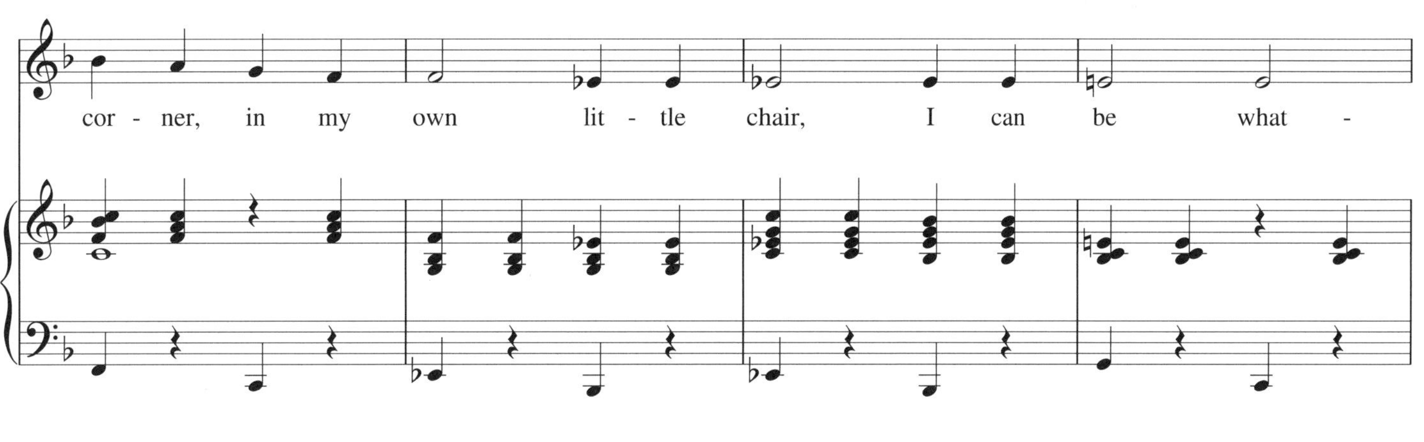
cor - ner, in my own lit - tle chair, I can be what -

3
ev - er I want to be.
On the wing of my

fan - cy I can fly an - y - where And the world will

3
o - pen its arms to me.
I'm a

young Nor - we - gian prin - cess or a milk maid,
I'm the
great - est pri - ma don - na in Mi - lan,
I'm an
heir - ess who has al - ways had her silk made
By her
own flock of silk - worms in Ja - pan!
I'm a

girl men go mad for, Love's a game I can play With a
cool and con- fi- dent kind of air,
3
Just as
long as I stay in my own lit - tle cor - ner,
All a -
lone in my own lit - tle chair.

I can
be what - ev - er I want to be.
I'm a
slave in Cal - cut - ta, I'm a queen in Pe - ru,
I'm a
mer - maid danc - ing up - on the sea.
I'm a
p
3

hunt - ress on an Af - ri - can sa - fa - ri (It's a

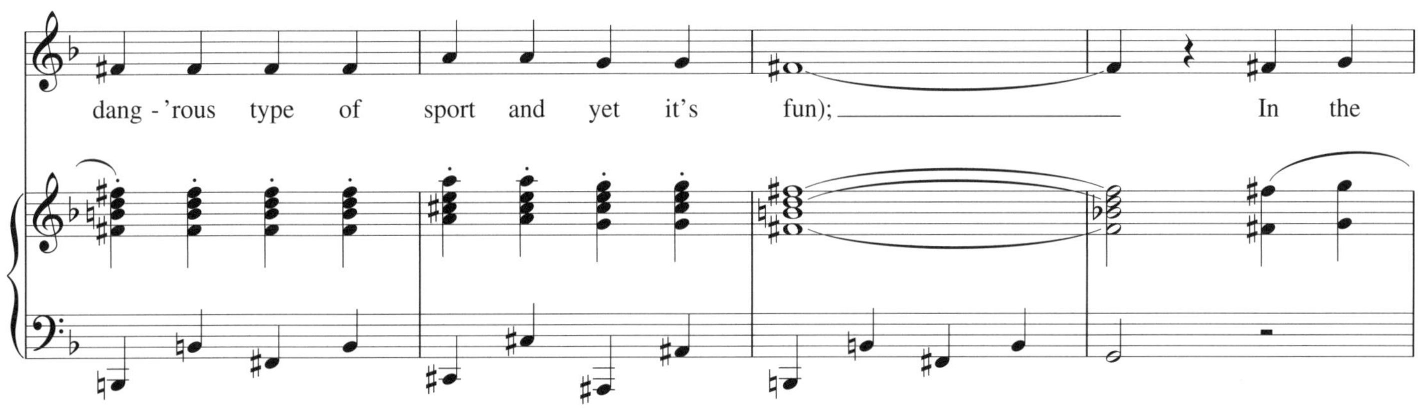
dang - 'rous type of sport and yet it's fun); In the

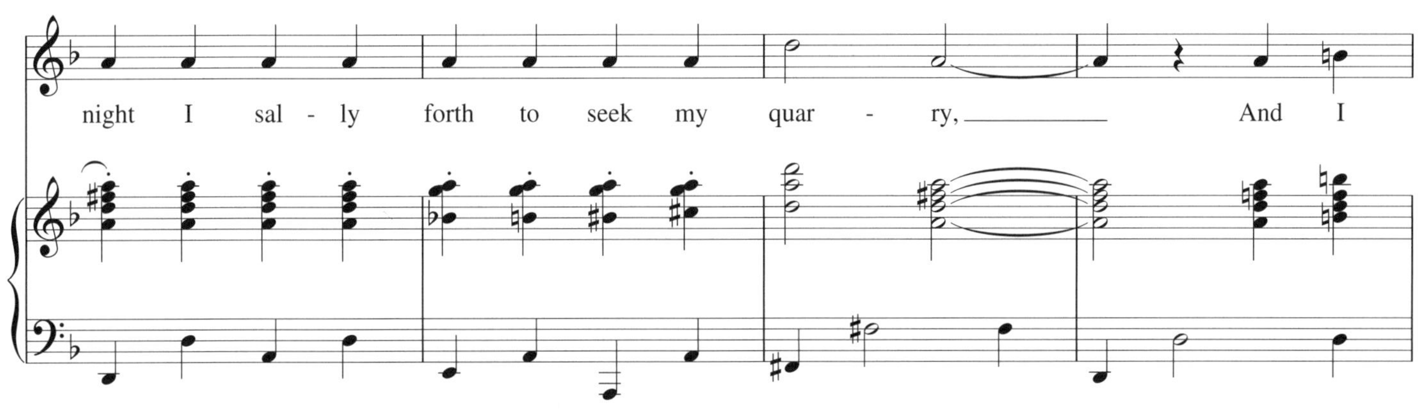
night I sal - ly forth to seek my quar - ry, And I

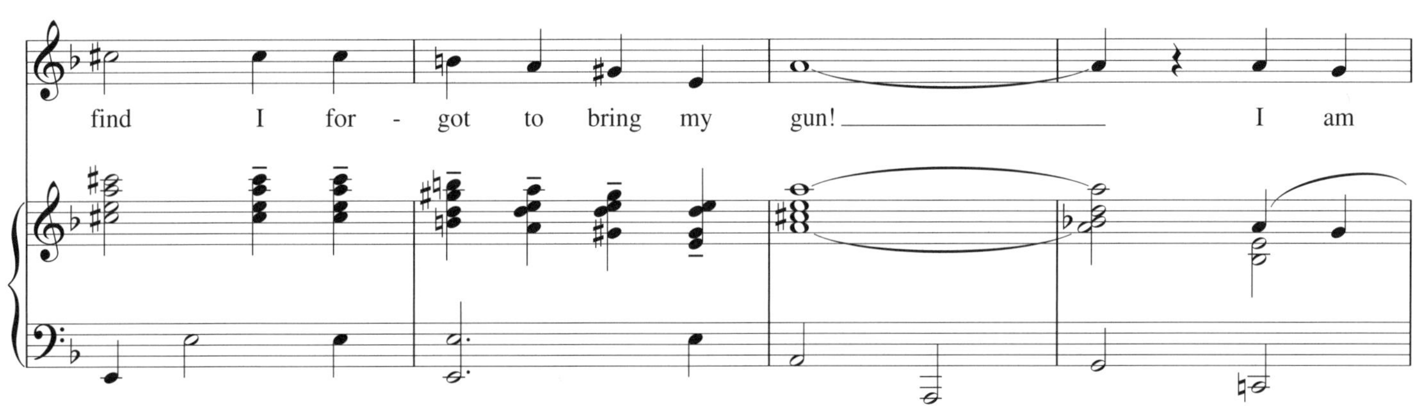
find I for - got to bring my gun! I am

lost in the jun - gle All a - lone and un - armed When I
meet a li - on - ess in her lair!
3
Then I'm
Slower
glad to be back in my own lit - tle cor - ner,
rit.
All a -
lone in my own lit - tle chair.
p

IS IT REALLY ME?

from *110 in the Shade*

Lyrics by Tom Jones
Music by Harvey Schmidt

see.
Some - one who is beau - ti - ful;
Is it real - ly me?
Mo-ments a - go,
I was a - lone
hop-ing that this could be.
Now here I am,
safe in your arms.
And I'm no long - er lone - ly.
3
mp
fp
rit.
pp

a tempo
Is it real - ly me?
Is it real - ly
p
a tempo
cresc.
true?
Sud-den-ly I'm beau-ti-ful
all be-cause of
poco a poco
mf
you.
Sud-den-ly I'm beau - ti - ful
Freely
beau-ti-ful with
8va
loco
f
mp
Slowly - In tempo
you.
8va
loco
mf
f rall.
ff

IT WONDERS ME

from *Plain and Fancy*

Lyrics by Arnold B. Horwitt
Music by Albert Hague

day can be, So green the field, So blue the sky,
So red and gold the map - le tree.
Some-where a breeze be - gins to sing Some-where a bird
is an - swer-ing, So won-der-ful sweet the

mel - o - dy,
It won-ders me.
mf
p
So green the field,
So blue the sky,
So
gold the tree,
It won-ders me.
mp

So green the field,
So blue the sky,
So red and gold the ma - ple tree,
Some-where a breeze be - gins to sing
Some-where a bird is an - swer - ing,
p
p
3

So wonder-ful sweet the mel-o-dy,
It won-ders me.
So green the field,
So blue the sky,
So gold the tree,
It won-ders me.
mf
ff

LOVELY

from *A Funny Thing Happened on the Way to the Forum*

Words and Music by
Stephen Sondheim

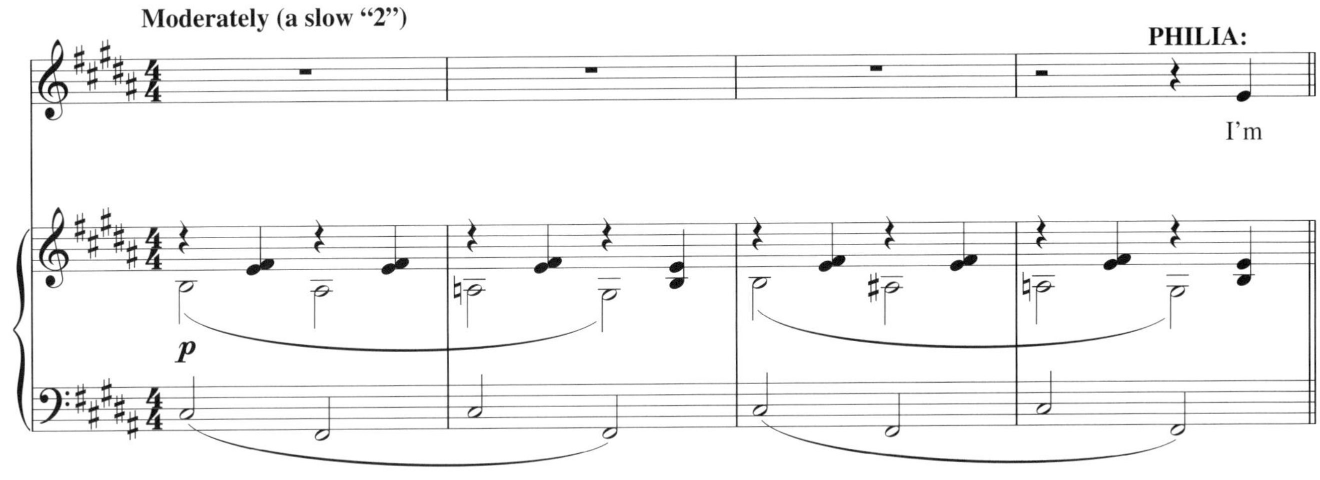

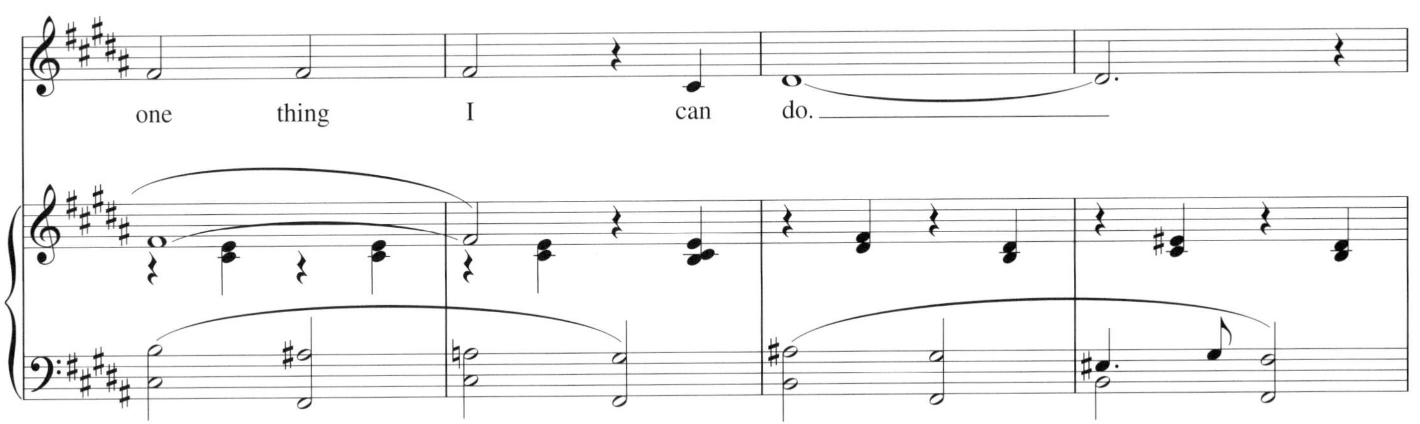

Win - some,
What I am is win - some,
ra - di - ant as
in some dream come true.
Oh,
Is - n't it a shame
I can nei - ther
sew, Nor cook, nor read or write my name.
rall.
But I'm
rall.

a tempo
hap - py Mere-ly be-ing love - ly, For it's
a tempo
one thing I can give to you.
poco rall.
a tempo
I'm love - ly, All I am is
p
love - ly. Love-ly is the one thing I can

do.
Win - some,
What I am is
win - some,
Ra - di - ant as in some dream come
true.
Oh,
Is - n't it a
shame
I can nei - ther sew,
Nor cook,
nor read or write my

ten. ten.
name. And I'm hap - py, Hap-py that I'm
ten. ten.
mp
love - ly, For there's one thing love-li - ness can
do: It's a gift for me to share with
p
you.
3
slowly
f

MAKE BELIEVE

from *Show Boat*

Lyrics by Oscar Hammerstein II
Music by Jerome Kern

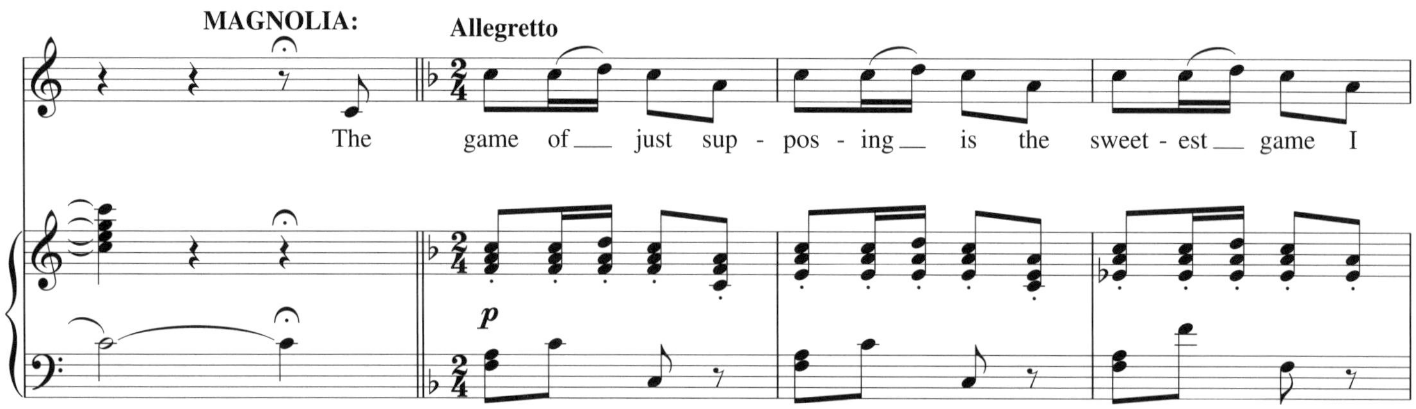

This song is a duet for Magnolia and Ravenal in the show, adapted as a solo for this edition.

see.
And if the things we dream a - bout don't hap - pen to be
so,
That's just an un - im - port - ant tech - ni - cal - i -
ty.
Poco animato (𝅗𝅥 = ♩)
Tho' the cold and bru - tal fact is
You and I have nev - er met,
We need not

mind con - ven - tion's P's and Q's.
If we put our thoughts in prac - tice
We can ban - ish all re -
gret,
I - mag - in - ing most an - y -
thing we choose.
We could
p
p dolce

make be - lieve I love you, We could
make be - lieve that you love me. Oth - ers
find peace of mind in pre - tend - ing Could - n't
you? Could - n't I? Could - n't we Make be -

lieve our lips are blend - ing in a
phan - tom kiss, or two, or three
3
Might as
Ped.
cresc.
well make be - lieve I love you.
f
For, to
dim.
tell the truth, I
opt.
do.

MANY A NEW DAY

from *Oklahoma!*

Lyrics by Oscar Hammerstein II
Music by Richard Rodgers

man I lose is the on - ly man a-mong men. I'll snap my fin-gers to
show I don't care, I'll buy me a brand new dress to wear, I'll scrub my neck and I'll
rit.
rit.
brush my hair And start all o-ver a - gain.
a tempo
a tempo, con ritmo
Refrain
Con grazia - non legato
Man-y a new face will please my eye, Man-y a new love will find me,
p

Nev-er-'ve I once looked back to sigh o-ver the ro - mance be - hind me,
Man-y a new day will dawn be - fore I do!
Man-y a light lad may kiss and fly, A kiss gone by is by - gone,
Nev-er-'ve I asked an Au - gust sky, "Where has last Ju - ly gone?"

3
Nev- er - 've I wan - dered through the rye, Won-der - in' where has some
3
guy gone, Man-y a new day will dawn be - fore I do!
3
Nev-er-'ve I chased the hon - ey bee who care - less - ly ca -
3
3
joled me, Some-bod- y else just as sweet as he, cheered me and con -
3
3
L.H.

soled me. Nev-er-'ve I wept in - to my tea o-ver the deal some - one
doled me, Man-y a new day will dawn, Man-y a red sun will
set, Man-y a blue moon will shine, be - fore I
do!
(Should)
poco rit.
rit.
f a tempo

MUCH MORE

from *The Fantasticks*

Words by Tom Jones
Music by Harvey Schmidt

*small notes are optional throughout.

old! I'd like to be not e - vil, But a
mp
lit - tle world - ly wise. To be the kind of
girl de - signed To be kissed up - on the eyes. I'd
(Same tempo - non accel.)
like to dance till two o'-clock Or some-times dance till
pp poco a poco cresc.
(no pedal)

dawn, Or if the band could stand it, Just go
on and on and on! Just once! Just
(use pedal)
f
8va
f
once! Be - fore the chance is gone! I'd
8va
mp
f rit.
like to waste a week or two, And nev - er do a
mp
a tempo

chore. To wear my hair un - fast - ened So it
bil - lows to the floor.
A tempo (non accel.)
To do the things I've
8va
allarg.
poco rall.
pp poco a poco cresc.
(no pedal)
dreamed a - bout, But nev - er done be - fore. Per -
haps I'm bad, or wild, or mad, With lots of grief in

store, But I want much more than keep-ing house! Much
8va
loco
8va
f
f
mp
(use pedal)
more! Much more! Much
8va
f
allarg.
more!
loco
8va
loco
8va
ff a tempo
fff poco rit.

MY FAVORITE THINGS

from *The Sound of Music*

Lyrics by Oscar Hammerstein II
Music by Richard Rodgers

Cream col - ored pon - ies and crisp ap - ple
mf
mp
strud - els, Door - bells and sleigh - bells and schnitz - el with noo - dles,
Wild geese that fly with the moon on their wings, These are a
few of my fa - vor - ite things.
f

Girls in white dress - es with blue sat - in sash - es, Snow - flakes that
mf
stay on my nose and eye - lash - es, Sil - ver white win - ters that
melt in - to springs, These are a few of my fa - vor - ite things.
When the dog bites, When the bee stings,
mf

When I'm feel - ing sad,
I
sim - ply re - mem - ber my fa - vor - ite things and
then I don't feel so bad.
cresc.
f
sf

MY WHITE KNIGHT

from Meredith Willson's *The Music Man*

Words and Music by
Meredith Willson

Poco mosso
All I want is a plain man; All I want is a mod - est _ man; A
p
qui - et man, a gen - tle man, a straight - for - ward and hon - est man to
3
sit with me in a cot - tage _ some - where in the state of I - o - wa. ___ And I would like him to
p
be ___ more in - t'rest - ed in me ___ than he is in him -
ten.

self. And more in-t'rest-ed in us than in me.
Poco lento
ten.
And if oc-ca-sion-'ly he'd pon - der what makes Shake-speare and Bee-thov-en great,
pp
Lento
him I could love 'til I die.
Molto lento
Him I could love 'til I die.
Tempo I
My white knight, not a Lanc-e-lot nor an an-gel with wings;
p

Just some-one to love me, who is not a-shamed of a few nice things. My white
R.H.
R.H.
knight; let me walk with him where the oth-ers ride by; Walk, and love him
Very broadly
Molto lento
Tempo I
Ossia
'til I die. 'Til I die.
poco cresc.
f
molto cresc.
ff
sfz

NO OTHER LOVE

from *Me and Juliet*

Lyrics by Oscar Hammerstein II
Music by Richard Rodgers

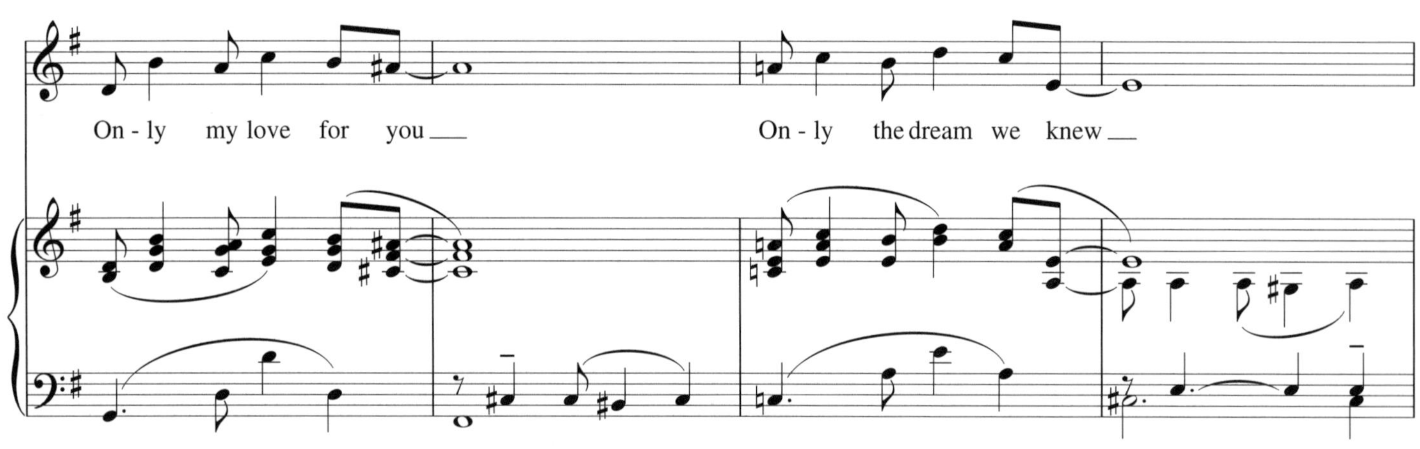

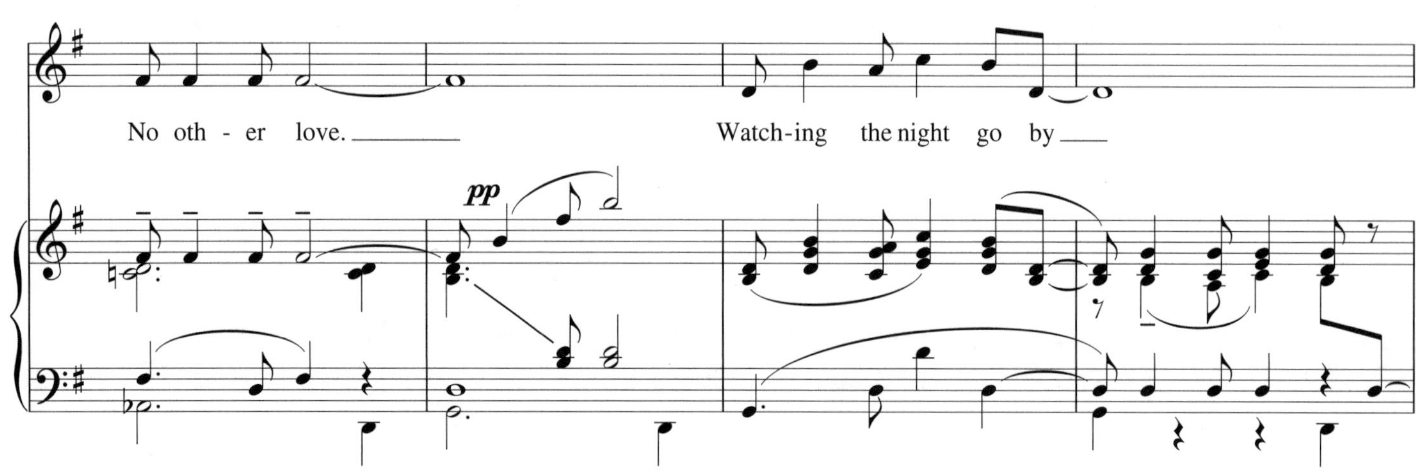

Wish - ing that you could be
Watch-ing the night with me,
In - to the night I cry:
Hur - ry home, come
home to me!
Set me
free,
free from doubt and

free from long - ing. In - to your arms I'll fly.
mf
Locked in your arms I'll stay,
Wait - ing to hear you say:
No oth - er love have
I, No oth - er love.
rit.
cresc.
sf

ONCE YOU LOSE YOUR HEART

from *Me And My Girl*

Words and Music by
Noel Gay

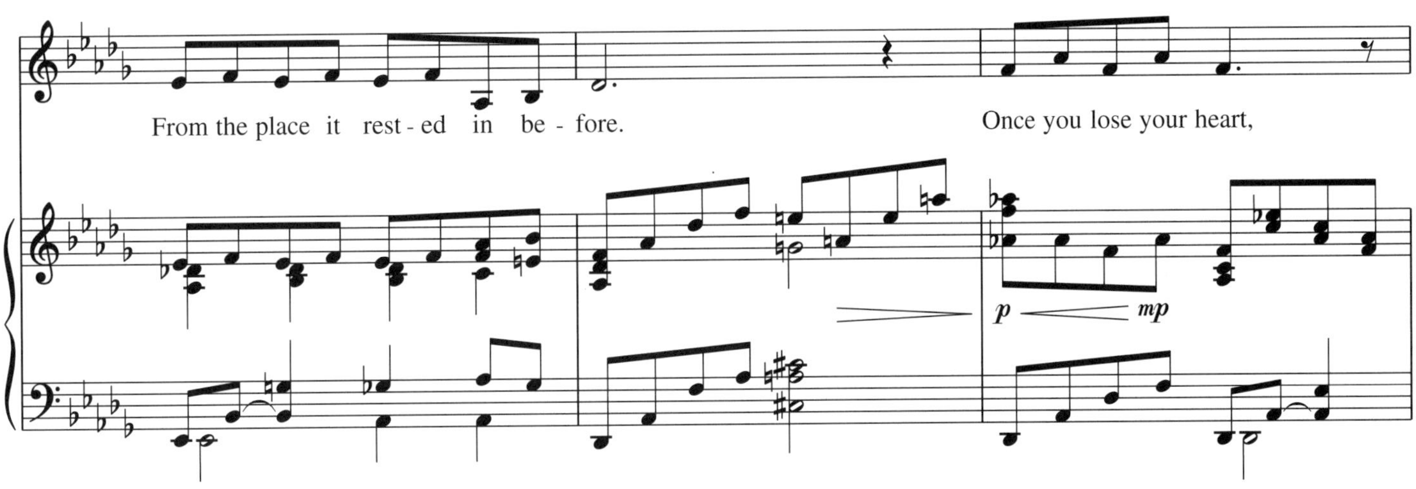

gone be - fore you knew it could ev - er go that way, And
mf
rall. e dim.
now you must pur - sue it for - ev - er and a day.
a tempo
Once you lose your heart,
rall. e dim.
a tempo
Once some-bod - y takes it,
accel.
There's one thing cer-tain from the start,
rall.
you'll find for -
accel. e cresc.
rall.
ev - er, You've got to fol - low your heart.
They

più mosso
say a girl should nev - er be with - out love, And
più mosso
all the joy that love a - lone can bring. All that I have ev - er learnt a -
cresc.
bout love, tells me it's a ver - y fun-ny thing. For
3
dim.
accel.
when your heart is fan - cy - free, You hope some man will choose it, But

poco rall.
oh the spin you find you're in, The ver - y mo-ment that you lose it.
poco rall.
Tempo Primo
Once you lose your heart, Once some-bod - y takes it, From the place it rest-ed in be -
fore. Once you lose your heart, Once some-bod - y takes it,
poco più mosso
Then it is - n't your heart an - y more. It's gone be-fore you knew it could
poco accel.
mf

rall.
ev - er go that way, And now you must pur - sue it for - ev - er and a day.
rall. e dim.
Tempo Primo
Once you lose your heart, Once some-bod - y takes it, There's one thing cer - tain from the
poco accel.
rall.
start, You've got to fol - low, You've got to
rall. al fine
f
fol - low your heart.
mp
dim.
8vb

OUT OF MY DREAMS

from *Oklahoma!*

Lyrics by Oscar Hammerstein II
Music by Richard Rodgers

dreams and in - to the hush of fall - ing shad -
ows, When the mist is low and stars are
break - ing through. Then out of my dreams I'll go
Into a dream with
p

you.
Won't have to make up an - y more sto - ries
mf
You'll be there!
Think of the bright
mid - sum - mer night glo - ries we can

share.
Won't have to go on kiss-ing a day -
dream I'll have you
You'll
be real
Real as the white moon light-ing the
blue.
Out of my
poco rit.
p a tempo

dreams and in - to your arms, I long to fly
I will come as eve - ning comes to woo a
wait - ing sky.
Out of my dreams and
in - to the hush of fall - ing shad - ows

When the mist is low and stars are break - ing
through Then out of my dreams I'll go
opt.
In - to a dream with
you.

THE SIMPLE JOYS OF MAIDENHOOD

from *Camelot*

Words by Alan Jay Lerner
Music by Frederick Loewe

must ad-mit I've al-ways been a lamb. But Gen-e-vieve, St. Gen-e-vieve, I
Allegro
(with vehement rebellion)
won't o-bey you an-y-more! You've gone a bit too far. I won't be bid and
pp
bar-gain'd for Like beads at a ba-zaar. St. Gen-e-vieve, I've run a-way, E-
lud-ed them and fled, And from now on I in-tend to pray to some-one else in-

stead.
f
Moderato
(plaintively)
Oh, Gen - e- vieve! St. Gen - e- vieve! Where were you when my youth was
mf
p
sold? Dear Gen - e- vieve, sweet Gen - e- vieve, Shan't I be young be - fore I'm
Allegro
old?
mf
poco rall.

Allegretto
rall.
pp
Where are the sim - ple joys of maid - en - hood?
Where are all those a - dor - ing, dar - ling boys?
Where's the knight pin - ing so for me He leaps to death in woe for me? Oh,
where are a maid - en's sim - ple joys?
Shan't

I have the nor - mal life a maid - en should? Shall I
pp
nev - er be res - cued in the wood? Shall two
knights nev - er tilt for me And let their blood be spilt for me? Oh,
where are the sim - ple joys of maid - en - hood?

Shall I not be on a ped - es - tal,
Wor - shipped and com - pet - ed for?
Not be car-ried off, or bet - ter still,
Cause a lit - tle war?
poco rall.
Where are the sim - ple joys of maid - en - hood?
Are those
a tempo
sweet, gen - tle pleas - ures gone for good?
Shall a

feud not be - gin for me? Shall kith not kill their kin for me? Oh,
where are the triv - ial joys...? Harm - less, con - viv - ial joys...?
Where are the sim - ple joys of maid - en - hood?
poco rall.
Poco più mosso
mf
f

SIMPLE LITTLE THINGS

from *110 in the Shade*

Lyrics by Tom Jones
Music by Harvey Schmidt

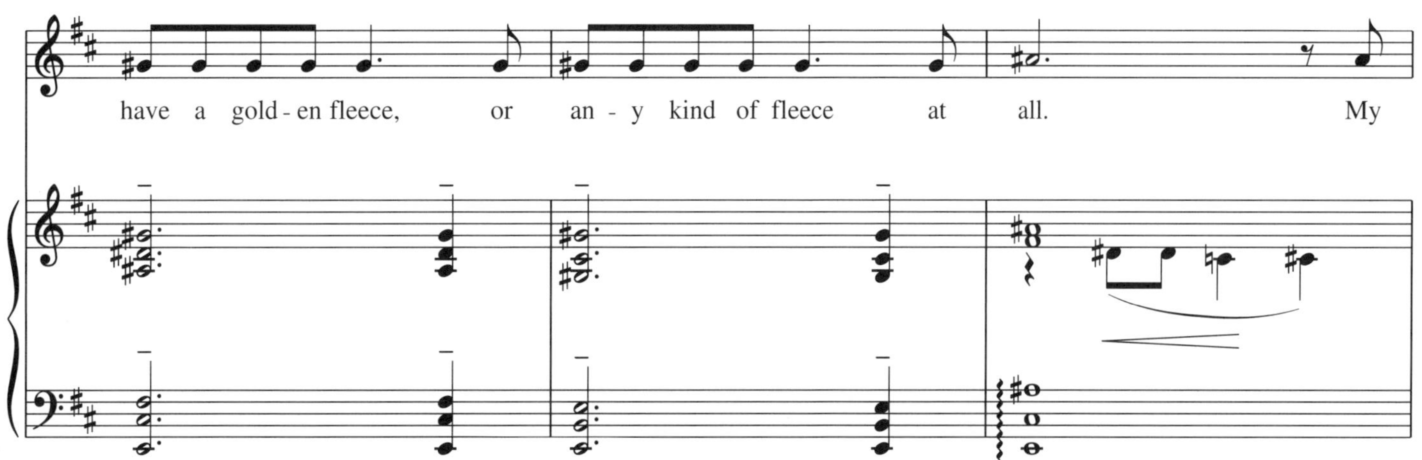

dreams, like my name, are ver - y plain; no shin - ing knight must kneel. My
mp
dreams, like my name, are ver - y plain; but nev - er - the - less, they're
3
real. They're all so ver - y real.
p
poco rall.

Slowly - Rubato
Sim-ple lit-tle things.
All I want are
sim-ple lit-tle things.
pp
L.H.
Tempo - Slow 4
All I need is
some - one be - side me to
pp
11
have and to hold,
some - one to love me as
we grow old - er.
Sim-ple lit-tle things,

Sim-ple lit - tle dreams, will do.
poco rall.
"Liz-zie, is my blue suit pressed?
Liz - zie, kind - a' scratch be-tween my shoul-der blades.
pp
Liz-zie, are the
chil - dren all in bed?"
That's what he'll say,
I'll say: "My hus - band."
rit.

Sim-ple lit-tle things.
All I want are
sim-ple lit-tle things.
a tempo
All I need is
some-one be-side
me to
have and to hold,
some-one to love
me as
we
grow
old - er.
Sim-ple lit-tle things,
ten.
Very slow, in 8
sim-ple lit-tle dreams,
will
do.
8va
rit.
p

SIXTEEN GOING ON SEVENTEEN

from *The Sound of Music*

Lyrics by Oscar Hammerstein II
Music by Richard Rodgers

go - ing on sev - en - teen, In - no - cent as a rose.
Bach - e - lor dan - dies, drink - ers of bran - dies, what do I know of
those? To - tal - ly un - pre - pared am I To
mp
face a world of men. Tim - id and shy and

scared am I of things be - yond my ken.
gliss.
I need some - one old - er and wis - er Tell - ing me what to
mf
deciso
do.
mf
You are sev - en - teen, go - ing on eight - een,
I'll de - pend on you.

SO MANY PEOPLE

from *Saturday Night*

Music and Lyrics by
Stephen Sondheim

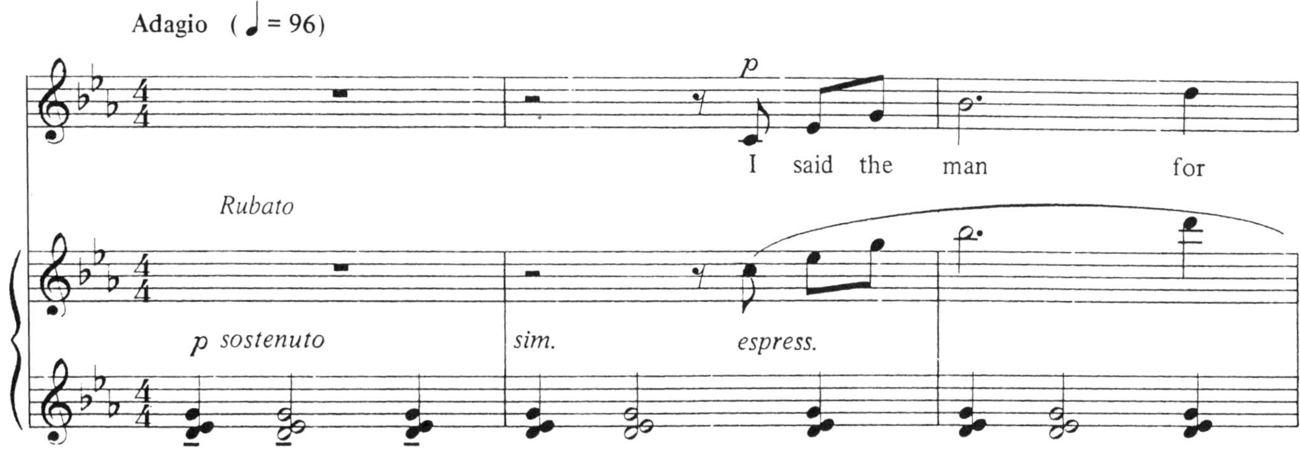

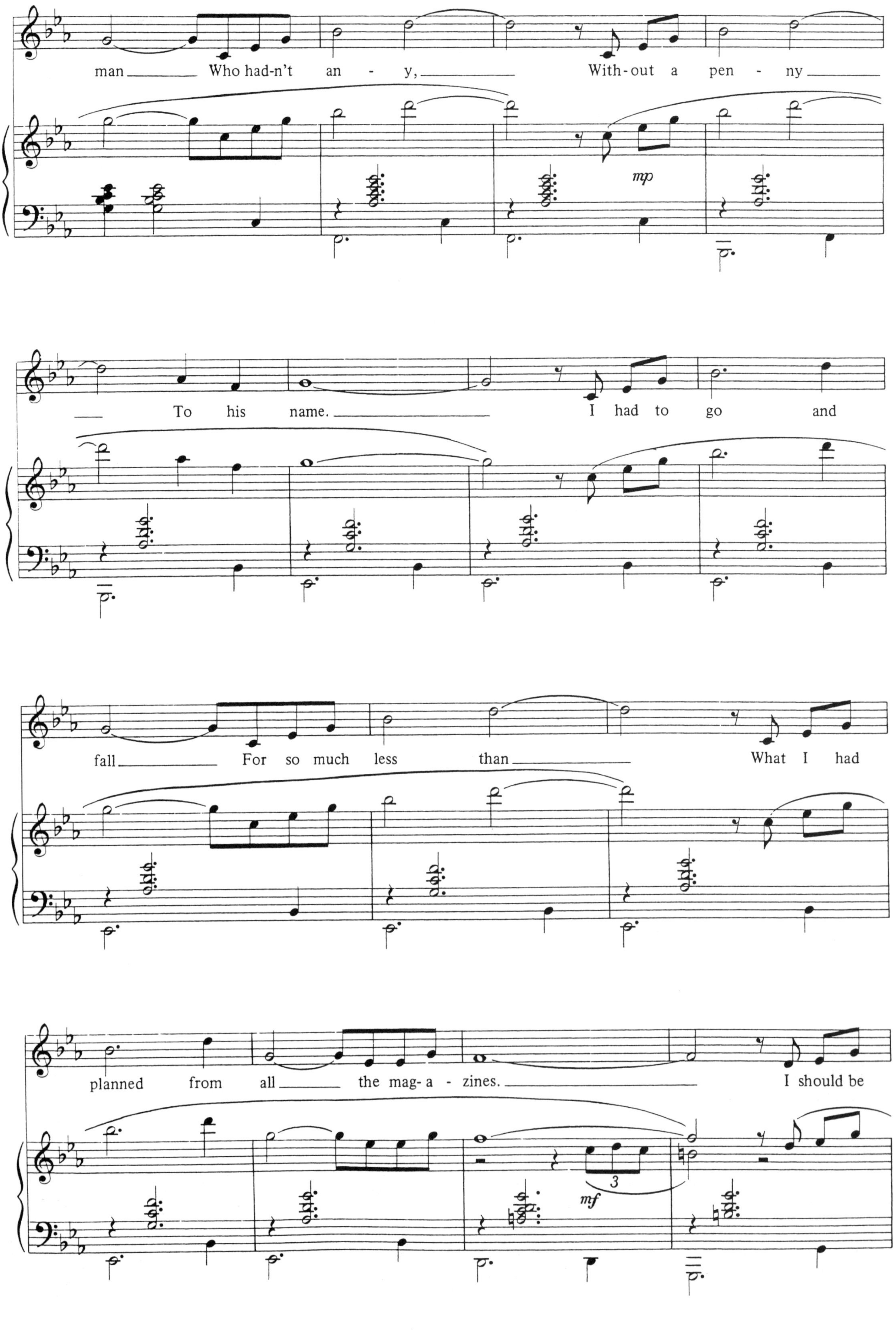
man Who had-n't an - y, With-out a pen - ny
mp
To his name. I had to go and
fall For so much less than What I had
planned from all the mag- a - zines. I should be
mf
3

cresc.
good and sore: What am I hap - py for? I guess the
dim.
man means more Than the means.
dim.
mp
Non rubato (𝅗𝅥 = 48)
So man-y peo - ple in the world, And
3
what can they do? They'll nev - er know love Like

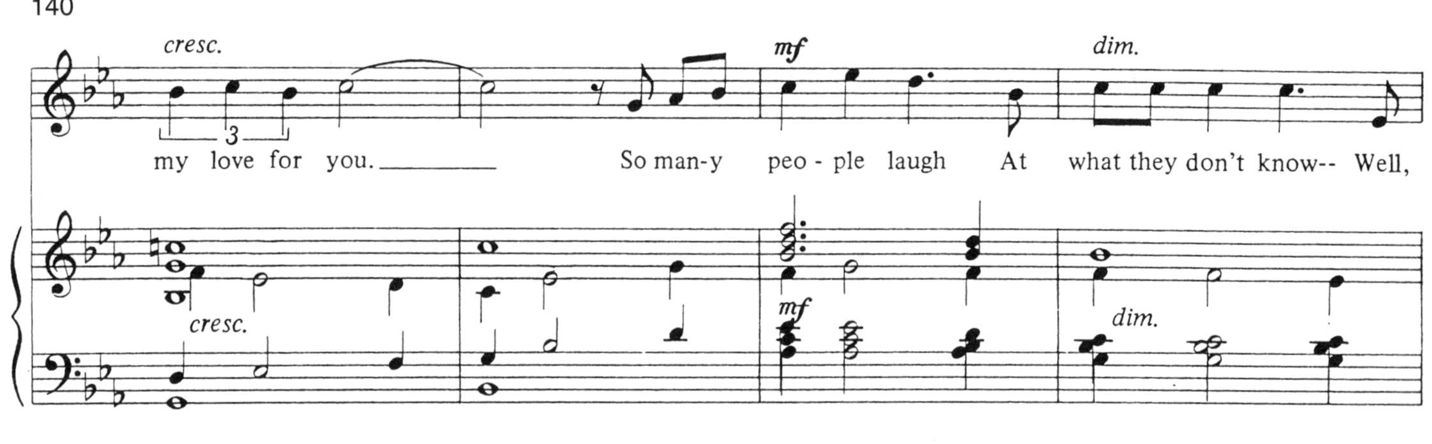
cresc.
mf
dim.
my love for you. So man-y peo-ple laugh At what they don't know-- Well,
cresc.
mf
dim.

mp
that's their con-cern. If just a few, say half a mil-lion or so, Could
mp

rit.
a tempo
see us, they'd learn. So man-y peo-ple in the
rit.
mf
a tempo

world Don't know what they've missed. They'd

never believe
Such
joy could exist.
cresc.
8va
f
loco
And if they tell us It's a thing we'll outgrow, They're
8va
loco
dim.
rall.
a tempo
jealous as they can be
That with so many people in the world You love
mp
rall.
a tempo
rit.
me!
mf
rit.

THE SOUND OF MUSIC

from *The Sound of Music*

Lyrics by Oscar Hammerstein II
Music by Richard Rodgers

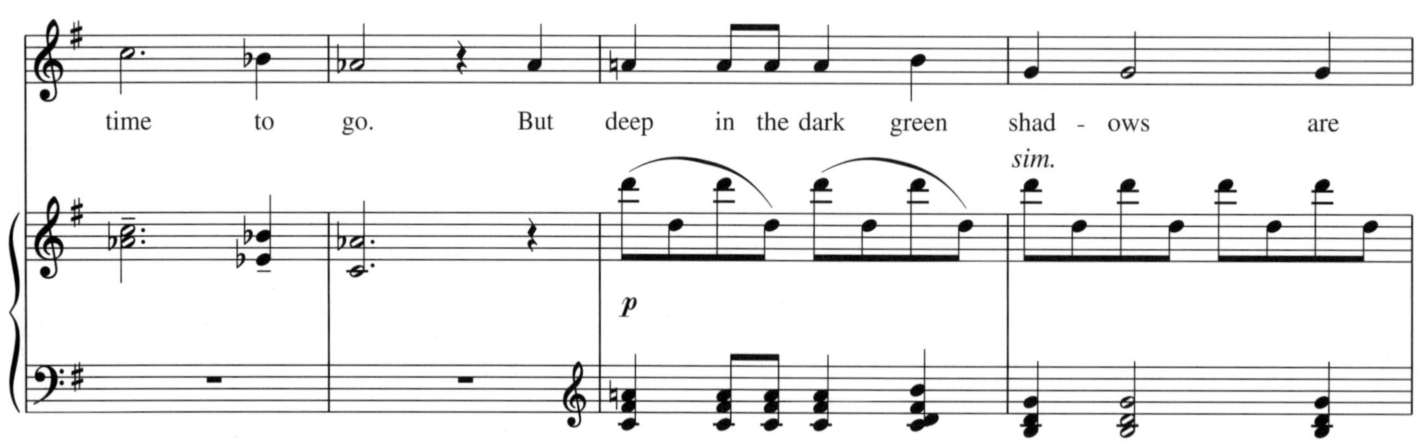

voic - es that urge me to stay. So I pause and I wait and I
lis - ten for one more sound, for one more love - ly thing that the
Con espressione
hills might say. The hills are a - live with the sound of
espr. p
mf p
mu - sic, with songs they have sung for a thou - sand

years. The hills fill my heart with the sound of
mu - sic. My heart wants to sing ev - 'ry song it
hears. My heart wants to beat like the wings of the birds that rise from the
lake to the trees. My heart wants to sigh like a chime that flies from a

church on a breeze, To laugh like a brook when it trips and falls o - ver
stones in its way, To sing through the
night like a lark who is learn - ing to pray. I
go to the hills when my heart is lone - ly.
f
p

I know I will hear what I've heard be - fore.
My heart will be blessed with the sound of mu - sic
And I'll sing once more.
colla voce

THERE'S A SMALL HOTEL

from *On Your Toes*

Words by Lorenz Hart
Music by Richard Rodgers

poco rit.
Where fun - ny peo - ple can have fun. That's where we two will
In 4
Meno
(rhythmically strict)
go, Dar - ling, Be - fore you can count up one, two,
Allegretto, in 2 (𝅗𝅥 = 56)
three. For: There's a small ho - tel with a
wish - ing well; I wish that we were there to - geth - er.

There's no bri - dal suite: One room
bright and neat, Com - plete for us to share to -
geth - er. Look - ing through the win - dow you can
see a dis - tant stee - ple: Not a sign of peo - ple,

Tempo I
Who wants
peo - ple?
When the
p
stee - ple bell
says,
"Good - night,
sleep well,"
We'll thank
the small ho -
tel
to - geth - er.
Pret - ty win - dow cur - tains
made of chintz
In our make be - lieve land.

On the wall are sev - 'ral
cheer - ful prints Of Grant and Grov - er Cleve - land. Go
down in - to the par - lor and feast your eyes On the moose - head on the
wall. Per - haps you'd like to play the or - gan,

They tune it ev - 'ry oth - er fall.
The gar-den
ppp
will be like
Ad-am and Eve - land.
No, they
3
nev - er did go in for car - riage trade;
They get what is known as mar - riage trade!
rall.
Oh,

Tempo I
p
When the stee - ple bell says, "Good -
night, sleep well, you ver - y small ho - tel," We'll creep in -
(Slower)
7
In 4
molto rall.
to our lit - tle shell And we will thank the small ho -
tel to - geth - er.
pp
L.H.
R.H.

THINK OF ME

from *The Phantom of the Opera*

Music by Andrew Lloyd Webber
Lyrics by Charles Hart
Additional Lyrics by Richard Stilgoe

try.
On that day, that not so dis - tant day, when you are
far a - way and free,
if you ev - er find a
mo - ment,
spare a thought for
me.
f

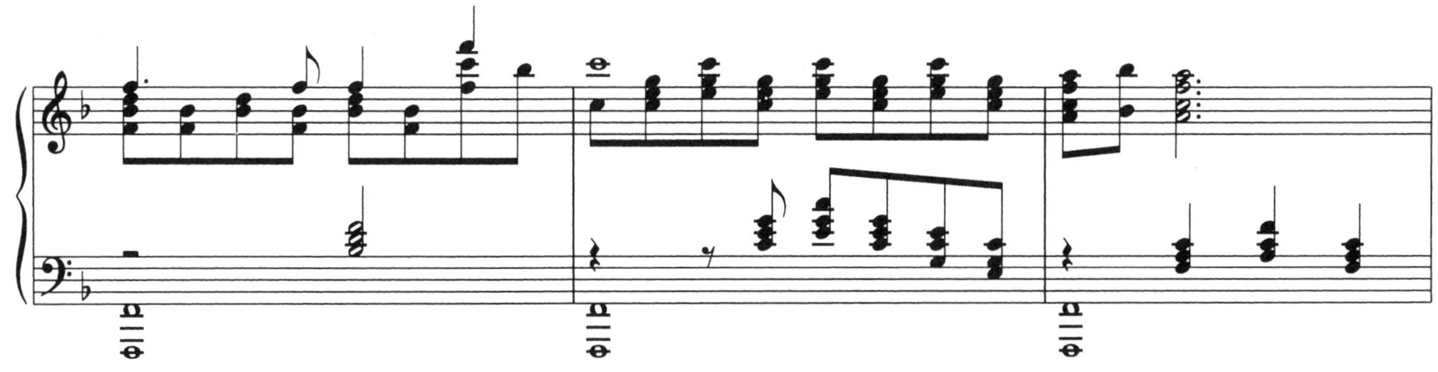

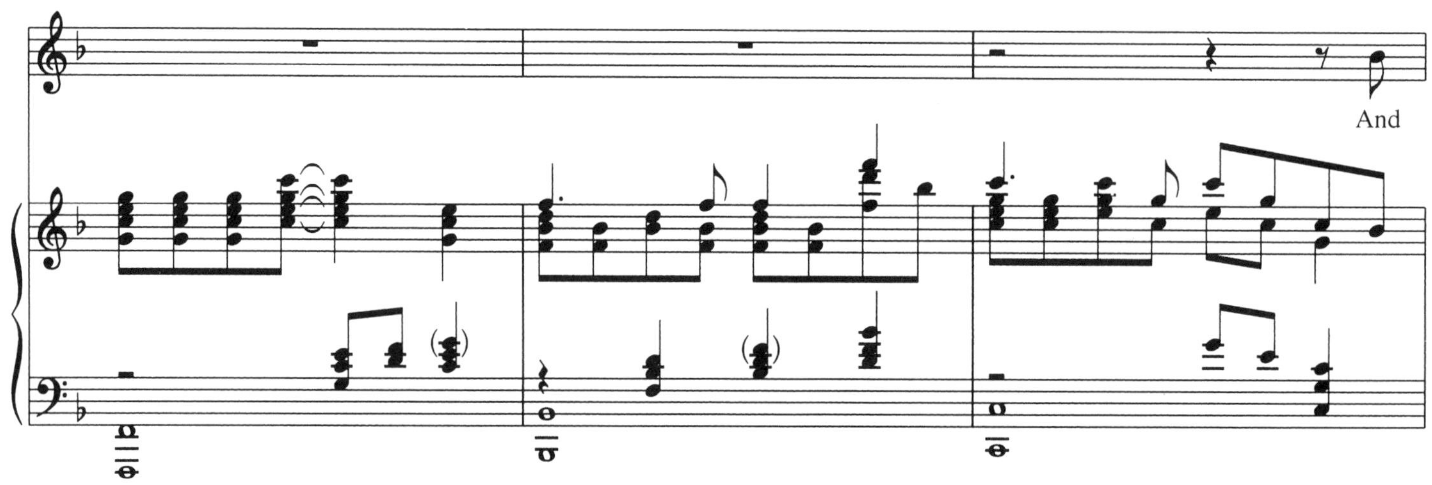
And

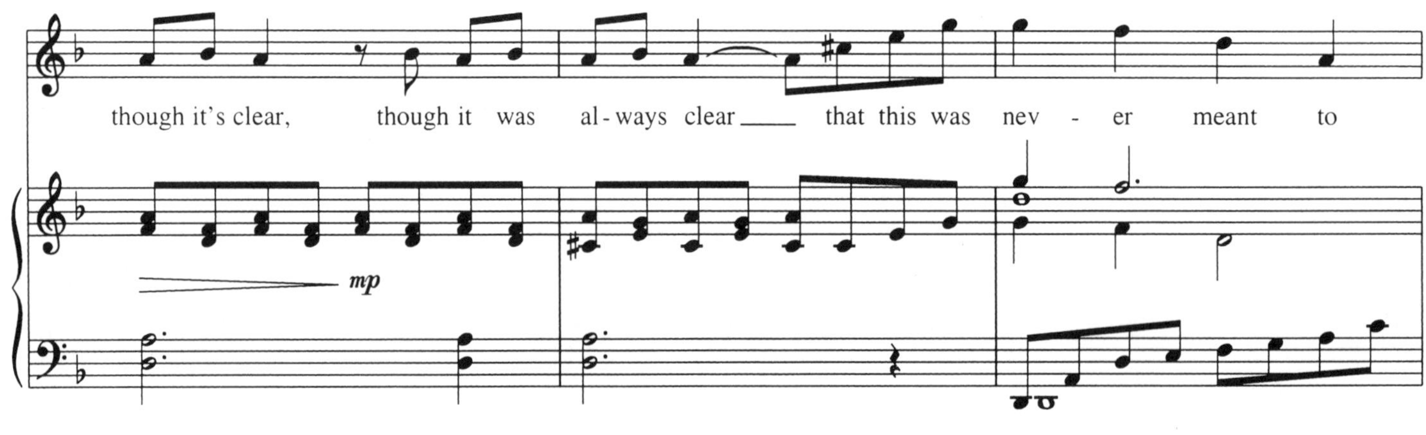
though it's clear, though it was al-ways clear that this was nev - er meant to
mp

be, if you hap-pen to re - mem - ber,
12
8

stop and think of me. Think of
Au - gust when the trees were green; don't
think a - bout the way things might have
poco rit.
A Tempo
been. Think of me, think of me wak - ing
poco rit.

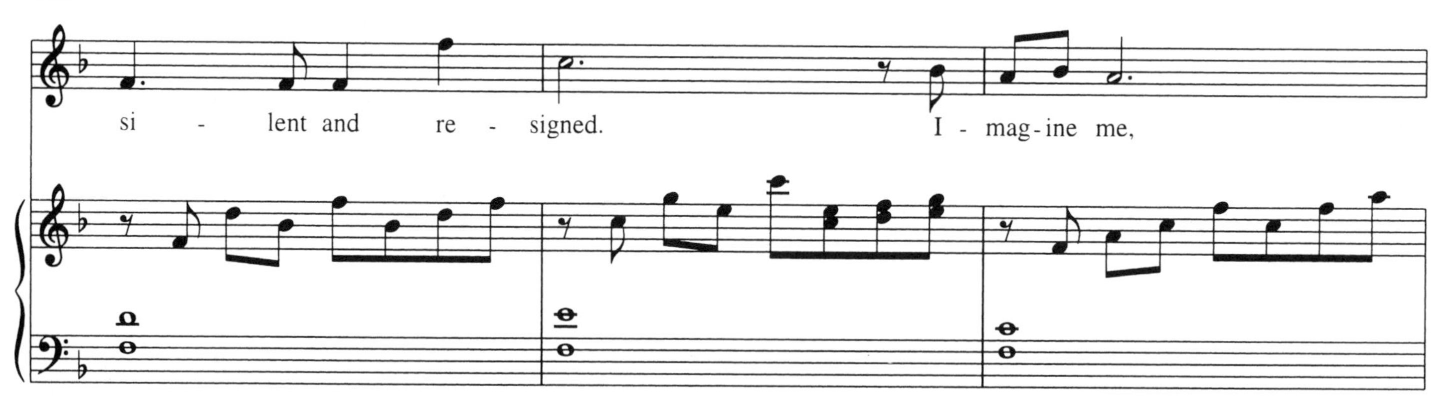
si - lent and re - signed. I - mag - ine me,

try - ing too hard _ to put you from my mind.

Think of me _____ please say you'll think of me _____ what - ev - er else you choose to

no rit.
do. There will nev - er be a day when
no rit.

poco più mosso
I won't think of you.
ff
mp
f
Flow-ers fade, the fruits of sum-mer fade, they have their

sea - son so do we... but please prom - ise me that

cadenza
some - times you will think ah

ah
ah

of me!
f
fp
ff

WITHOUT YOU

from *My Fair Lady*

Lyrics by Alan Jay Lerner
Music by Frederick Loewe

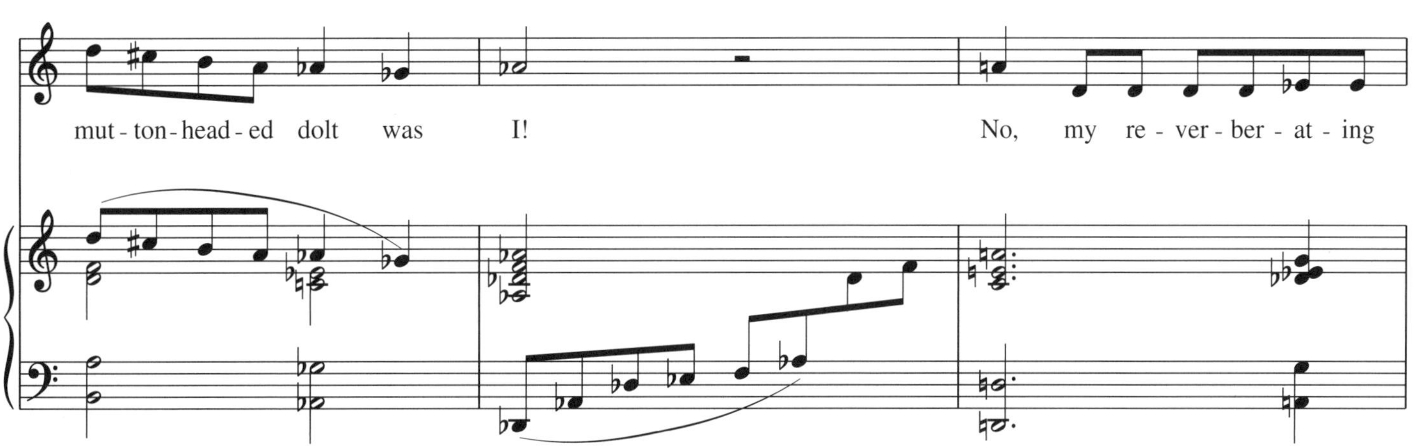

friend, You are not the be - gin - ning and the end! There'll be
Allegro con moto
spring ev - 'ry year with - out you. Eng - land still will be here with - out
you. There'll be fruit on the tree; and a shore by the sea; there'll be
crum - pets and tea with - out you. Art and mu - sic will thrive with - out
p
p

you. Some-how Keats will sur-vive with-out you. And there
still will be rain on that plain down in Spain, e-ven that will re-main with-out
you. I can do with-out
mf
you. You, dear friend, who talk so
p

well, you can go to Hart - ford, Her-es-ford and
Hamp - shire. They can still rule the land with-out you. Wind-sor Cas - tle will stand with-out
you. And with - out much a - do we can all mud - dle through with - out
you. With - out your pull-ing it, the tide comes in; with -
Poco meno
f
p
mf dim.
sf

poco rall.
out your twirl-ing it, the earth can spin. With - out your push-ing them, the clouds roll by. If
sf
p
poco rall.
Tempo giusto
they can do with-out you, duck-y, so can I! I shall
Tempo I
not feel a - lone with - out
sf p
you. I can stand on my own with-out you. So go
f
p
back in your shell, I can do blood-y well with-out you!
f

TILL THERE WAS YOU

from Meredith Willson's *The Music Man*

By Meredith Willson

you.
There were birds
in the sky,
but I
R.H.
nev - er
saw
them wing - ing.
No I
nev - er
saw them at
all,
till there was
3
3
3
you.
And there was
mu - sic
and
there
were
won - der - ful
3
L.H.
col voce
ro - ses,
they
tell
me,
in
sweet
frag - rant
mea - dows
of
R.H.

dawn and dew. There was love all a-round, but I

R.H.

p

nev - er heard it sing - ing. No, I nev - er heard it at all, till there was

3 3 3

you.

mp *mf* 3

sempre cresc.

3

f

cresc. molto

There was love all a-
round, but I nev-er heard it sing-ing. No, I
nev-er heard it at all, till there was you.
L.H.
p
col voce
rit.
molto espressivo
a tempo
f
mf
rit.
ad lib. trem.
molto rit.

WE KISS IN A SHADOW

from *The King and I*

Lyrics by Oscar Hammerstein II
Music by Richard Rodgers

This song is a duet for Lun Tha and Tuptin, adapted as a solo for this edition.

When peo - ple are near, we speak not a word.
A - lone in our se - cret,
To - geth - er we sigh
For
one smil - ing day to be free,
To kiss in the sun - light
And say to the sky:
7

Be - hold and be - lieve what you see!
Be - hold how my lov - er loves me!
A - lone in our se - cret,
To - geth - er we sigh
For one smil - ing day to be free,
pp

To kiss in the sun - light
And say to the sky:
Be - hold and be -
lieve what you see!
Be - hold how my
lov - er loves me!
7
rit.
pp a tempo
rit.
8va

WHAT'S THE USE OF WOND'RIN'

from *Carousel*

Lyrics by Oscar Hammerstein II
Music by Richard Rodgers

that.
Com-mon sense may tell you, That the
end - in' will be sad, And now's the time to break and run a -
way. But what's the use of won-d'rin' if the end - in' will be sad? He's your
fel - ler and you love him – There's noth-in more to say.
mf
p
mf

Some-thin' made him the way that he is, —
Wheth - er he's false — or true And some-thin' gave him the
things that are his — One of those things is you. So
when he wants your kiss - es you will give them to the lad, And
mp
mp
mf
p
3

an - y-where he leads you, you will walk and an - y-time he needs you, you'll go

run - nin' there like mad! You're his girl and he's your fel - ler

And all the rest is "talk!"

WISHING YOU WERE SOMEHOW HERE AGAIN

from *The Phantom of the Opera*

Music by Andrew Lloyd Webber
Lyrics by Charles Hart
Additional Lyrics by Richard Stilgoe

if I just dreamed, some-how you would be here.
Wish-ing I could hear your
voice a-gain,
know-ing that I nev - er would,
dream-ing of you won't help me to do
all that you dreamed I
could.
Pass - ing bells and sculpt - ed an-gels,

cold and mon - u - men - tal,
seem for you the wrong com-pan-ions;
rit.
a tempo
you were warm and gen-tle.
pp a tempo
rit.
3
Too man - y years
fight-ing back tears,
why can't the past just
die?
Wish-ing you were some - how
here a - gain;
ff

rall.
a tempo
3
knowing we must say good - bye.
Try to for - give,
teach me to live,
give me the strength to try.
ten. ten.
No more
a tempo
memories no more si - lent tears, no more gaz-ing a - cross the wast - ed
years. Help me say good - bye! Help me say good - bye!
molto rall.
mp
p
ff
8vb

WOULDN'T IT BE LOVERLY

from *My Fair Lady*

Words by Alan Jay Lerner
Music by Frederick Loewe

lots of heat; Warm face, warm hands, warm feet, oh, would - n't it be
lov - er - ly? Oh, so lov - er - ly sit - tin' ab - so-bloom - in' -
lute - ly still! I would nev - er budge 'til
Spring crept o - ver me win - der-sill Some - one's head rest - in'
mf dolce

on my knee; warm and ten - der as he can be,
Who takes good care of me; oh, would - n't
it be lov - er - ly? Lov - er - ly!
Lov - er - ly! Lov - er - ly! Lov - er - ly!
p
rall.
pp